# PIVOT
## to WIN

### Make the Big Plays In
### Life, Sports & Business

# PRAISE FOR
# *PIVOT TO WIN* AND
# JORDAN BABINEAUX

"I've been fortunate to get to know Jordan over the past few years. He radiates optimism, is fearless about change, and leans into opportunity. Like Jordan, I believe we all have the capacity for transformation throughout our lives, if we are willing to learn and act. The skills Jordan teaches in *Pivot to Win* provide a framework for anyone who wants to change where they are but can't figure out where to start, or how to make the most of their own personal or business pivots. I think everyone will find value in *Pivot to Win*."

—Bill Hilf, CEO, Vulcan Inc.

✗--->

"They say experience is the best teacher, and Jordan has that in life, sports, and business. I love the name of this book, *Pivot to Win*, as my brother has pivoted many times and continues to stack wins! From not landing a scholarship to a major university to going undrafted into the NFL to starting a career as a broadcaster and then starting his own business, it is incredible what Jordan has accomplished. Jordan possesses many traits that have led to his success; however, the two he always had on display were a relentless work ethic and an extremely optimistic attitude. Opportunity lies in challenges. As a teammate and competitor, he never backed down from a challenge and at times even seemed to enjoy it. Making the most of opportunities is what earned him the nickname "Big Play Babs." It should come as no surprise that the man who had a knack for pivoting a football game into a win is doing the same in life and business."

—Lofa Tatupu, former NFL linebacker, Seattle Seahawks

×--→

"*Pivot to Win* is a must-read for anyone pursuing challenging goals, a better life, or a desire to overcome difficult circumstances. Jordan Babineaux shows us how important the inner game is to winning—and offers clear, actionable techniques for mastering that game. He does this through a moving memoir that conveys his personal story and the deep motivation he has that fueled his success. Self-knowledge, self-awareness, and self-control are superpowers when it comes to winning, and Babineaux is the motivational coach to help you bring your all to the game."

—Marilyn Gist, Ph.D., former professor, University of Washington and Seattle University, author of *The Extraordinary Power of Leader Humility*

×--→

"I have had the pleasure of getting to know Jordan and watching his transition from an athlete to an entrepreneur, and what has always stood out to me is his truly authentic, relationship-based mindset. The fact that he is so passionate about helping others to understand and prepare for the transition from sports to business shows his true leadership ability. Jordan brings the perfect balance of personal commitment to excellence on and off the field and the natural ability to be an extremely effective communicator and connector for anyone who is lucky enough to have a chance to get to know him."

—Kris Naidu, CEO, Zeacon

×--→

"No one is more astute at capitalizing on adversity and change than an underdog—and Jordan Babineaux is the ultimate underdog. As an undrafted free agent, Jordan created a nearly decade-long career in the NFL and then started his career all over again, first as a broadcaster and second as an entrepreneur. Anyone who is committed to not only making the best of any situation but also knocking their goals out of the park must read *Pivot to Win*. I'm all about the underdog, and even though Jordan had an excellent NFL career, he continues to push himself to greatness as an underdog in the business world."

—John Schneider, general manager, Seattle Seahawks

×--->

"Jordan is a unique and accomplished individual in many ways, including reaching the most elite level of professional sports. And while his drive, personal story, and accomplishments are inspirational in many ways, his ability to recognize, dissect, and reconstruct the skills and habits that made him a professional athlete and apply them to "life after football" is truly motivating. It's great to give back financially, volunteer time, and help others. However, Jordan's ability to take his proven success in business, public speaking, and consistent personal improvement and share that with others as he does in *Pivot to Win* makes him a true leader in life."

—James Bocinsky, vice president, Private Wealth Management

×--->

"*Pivot to Win* is for you if you've ever been doubted, denied, or told you weren't good enough. Jordan Babineaux has been there, triumphed, and can now help you conquer your 'impossible' goals too. No excuses—get this book and get after it!"

—Darren Hardy, *New York Times* bestselling author and success mentor to CEOs and high achievers

×--->

"Jordan Babineaux is the essence of the pivot and has mastered it three times. *Pivot to Win* is a playbook for the tools and processes needed to harness your abilities learned through life. The opportunities are out there—let Jordan point you in the right direction."

—David Kirtman, executive director, J.P. Morgan Private Bank

×--->

"I have always felt that Jordan's story was one that needed to be fully explained to be believed. His inspirational story is one of faithful perseverance, and in *Pivot to Win* Jordan draws upon a wealth of experience in family, sports, and business to build a compelling case for self-assessment and improvement, especially in these uncertain times."

—Jason Jenkins, NFL executive, Miami Dolphins

×--→

"Having worked with Jordan Babineaux at NFL Network, I know first-hand how focused and adept he is at pivoting to conquer the task, no matter how daunting the challenge. We did live TV daily from 3 to 7 a.m. It was not easy. Not once did Jordan view this nocturnal lifestyle or our completely unpredictable cast as issues (we were). Instead, he parlayed things into greater opportunities. That's who he is. From earning his way onto an NFL roster from Southern Arkansas University to making one of the most memorable tackles in recent Seahawks memory, Jordan viewed challenges the way most of us view breathing—second nature. It's why he lasted so long in the NFL and why you won't hear anyone who has met him say anything but how humble, enjoyable, and promising he is. Then there is his family. From the one he came from in Texas to the one he now nurtures. I've watched him become the type of man we all aspire to be. While *Pivot to Win* is Jordan's chronicle and strategy for success, he's frankly just beginning to show us how potential can flourish into immeasurable human wealth."

—Steve Wyche, analyst, NFL Network

×--→

"Jordan Babineaux is the ultimate underdog who expects to win at anything he takes on and pushes himself to be successful. He proved this an undrafted free agent in the NFL who became a starter over a decade-long career. Post NFL, Jordan again proved it through a successful broadcasting career and as an entrepreneur. This book outlines his mindset, approach, and framework for making such successful transitions. I highly recommend it."

—Kevin M. Rabbitt, CEO, Hornblower Group

×--→

"As Jordan says, life is a series of pivots. We pivot from a state of sleep to wakefulness, work life to home life, and one job to another. We succeed when we learn how to take the difficult components of a pivot and spin them into gold. There's no better person to hear this from than a nine-year NFLer who was never expected to leave the small town of Port Arthur, Texas."

—Apolo Ohno, most decorated US male Winter Olympian of all time

×-->

"I have known Jordan Babineaux for the past few years. He is my fraternity brother, and I am a board member of one of his businesses.

Jordan is a very passionate, knowledgeable, and articulate individual. Jordan brings integrity and intelligence to all that he does. His ability to shift his career from performing at the highest level in the NFL to successfully becoming an NFL commentator to then starting and owning his successful businesses speaks to his intense drive and determination to always win in whatever he attempts to do. His belief that one can succeed with hard work and focus resonates with those who contact him.

His overall presence has had a positive impact on me and many others. Jordan's story needs to be shared for the masses to learn from. I endorse and recommend Jordan without reservation"

—Andre Corr, CEO, Waggle Solutions

×-->

"Undrafted free agents always know that their time's almost up. To stay in the league, they need copious amounts of grit, resilience, courage, and mental toughness. Jordan is always ready to do whatever it takes to get an invitation to the table, and when he's there he takes every opportunity that's offered to him. What Jordan's been able to achieve speaks to the character of the man and that character can help lead others to greatness."

—Maurice Kelly, vice president of Player Engagement, Seattle Seahawks

×-->

"Life has multiple chapters. Jordan Babineaux points out his own chapters from NFL player to broadcaster to business owner. How we pivot at these chapter changes helps to define our successes, not only in sports but also in growing businesses, career development, and relationships. When faced with challenges, plowing forward isn't always the best option—sometimes we need to spin and pivot, with new insights and perspective. A thoroughly engaging and inspiring read!"

—Karen Thomas, chairman, Seattle Sports Commission

x--->

"Through a series of small actions repeated over time, Jordan Babineaux beat the odds any person faces getting into the NFL. When his career ends, he has to start all over. First as a broadcaster and then as a business owner. In *Pivot to Win*, Jordan opens up about the mental fortitude and commitment any person needs to pivot their way to their best self."

—Walter Jones, Pro Football Hall of Fame Class of 2014, Seattle Seahawks

x--->

"Jordan Babineaux's vulnerability in sharing his own life story will draw you in from the first page. By the end of *Pivot to Win*, you'll be inspired to join his community of people forging their paths to their goals. As Jordan says: If you want more, become more. And the first step is picking up this book!"

—Curt Menefee, host, FOX NFL Sunday

x--->

"Jordan Babineaux is a true competitor in every sense of the word. Reading *Pivot to Win* will give you the same fire and passion Jordan has. This book gives you all the tools you need to feel empowered and achieve every goal in your life!"

—Nasser Kyobe (Nasa Chobie), executive producer, Seahawks Radio Network

**Insights & Inspiration from a Thought Leader,
NFL Star, Sports Analyst & Entrepreneur**

# PIVOT
## to WIN

**Make the Big Plays In
Life, Sports & Business**

# JORDAN BABINEAUX

Published by Oskie Press.

For ordering information or special discounts for bulk purchases as well as booking Jordan Babineaux to speak or host an event:

joinme@pivottowin.com
www.PivotToWin.com

Cover and Interior design by Kim Baker/Orange Brain Studio
Editing by Ivy Hughes
Copyediting by Alyssa Rabins
Composition by Accelerate Media Partners, LLC
ISBN: 978-1-7364761-0-9
Small Business/Entrepreneurship
Printed in the United States of America

# DEDICATION

*I dedicate this book to Mama. You kept us grounded in spirituality, education, and giving back.*

# TABLE OF

# CONTENTS

# PIVOTING, TRANSITIONING, AND WINNING

✖

## by Barbara Babineaux, Mom

Before the tragedy of Butch's unexpected death when Jordan was eight, I was prepared to grow old with the father of my children. I imagined that he and I would enjoy the success of our children as they moved through life's milestones—the graduations, the business ventures, the advancements in their respective careers, and the start of their families. But the vision I had of us sitting in rocking chairs waiting for the kids and grandkids to visit disappeared without any warning.

When Jordan talks about pivoting, transitioning, and winning, this is what he's talking about. He's talking about taking these unexpected, unplanned-for moments in life, accepting them, making the best of them, and becoming a better person because of them, not despite them. Acceptance is hard, though, especially when painful circumstances are the impetus behind a pivot or transition. After my kids' dad died, I had to spread myself thin. I wasn't just Mom anymore. I was Mom AND Dad, chef, counselor, doctor, lawyer, and primary breadwinner.

Even though I had to take on all of these roles, I was committed to building the foundation that Jordan's father and I had planned to build for our children. This meant putting them first—always. Adjusting to being everything for them while also grieving for my husband was heart-wrenching. Sometimes, the struggle became so unbearable that I thought I would never see my way out of the fog. "Lord," I'd ask, "how long will this continue overshadowing me?"

Every night, I would listen to gospel music to relax. For some reason, every time that I kneeled to pray, the Donnie McClurkin song "We Fall Down" would play. Then I started thinking: This song is for me, Lord. Thank you, thank you for my struggles. I knew that you would see me through this. I just had to wait, be still, and be patient.

Sometimes, things don't go the way we plan, but we can always find the right direction if we're patient and willing to look. Thankfully, I had God and the children's grandparents, aunts, uncles, and cousins to witness each of my kids' successes. Each one of these people provided guidance during a very dark period of my life.

Eventually, time helped me move through my grief, but so did my children. Watching them gave me great joy. I always wondered who would walk in their father's footsteps. Jeffery, my firstborn, assumed that since he was the oldest, he should be in charge, but Joshua, my second born, decided that he was going to be in charge because he was smart. Jean, my daughter, would keep everybody in line when I had to go to the grocery store. Jonathan and Jordan weren't worried about being in charge. They were more concerned with having fun. No matter what was going on, Jonathan and Jordan were always making up games or running around the house, or sliding down the second-story steps on a cardboard box sleigh. Just watching my children enjoy each other's company was enough joy for me.

Jordan and I have had to pivot and transition just like everyone else, but we're both better for it. In fact, I can honestly say that I do not have many regrets in life. I have made mistakes, I have experienced hardship and adversity, but I've also been given beautiful gifts. Even though the details may be different, this is all of our stories. We have to fight for the good things, the good people, and our faith. The one regret that I have is not finishing my bachelor's degree from Jarvis Christian College in Hawkins, Texas. If I had done that, I would have been the sixth Babineaux to graduate from college. I wish for this, but I'm sure proud of the five that graduated: My kids. All of my kids graduated from high school and college, and Jonathan, like Jordan, played in the NFL. I am truly proud of each of their accomplishments. We would not have made it through the fog without my faith.

Things have changed today, especially recently. People are being asked to dig into their grit and their resilience. They're being asked to change the way they live, the way they think, and the way they work, but every one of you reading *Pivot to Win* can do that. You can dig deep. You can break down the complicated things in your life into workable pieces so that you can succeed. You can work hard and accept your situation and be open to the things that will come. You can pivot, you can transition, and you can win.

Times will be hard and weary. Don't give up the fight! The fight will be long, and at times you will not be able to see your way through the fog, but keep going. Keep the faith. Be a leader. Even as a parent. Be generous with your hugs and smiles. In fact, use your smiles to get you through those hard times. Be patient, enjoy the life of your children that God has given you, keep the faith, keep your children in church, stay connected with each other, spend as much time as you can together, and—no matter how hard it is—love one another.

Sincerely,

*Barbara Babineaux*

Barbara Babineaux

---

*Author Note: I want to thank my mother for agreeing to talk about some very difficult experiences. This is the first time that she and I have spoken in depth about some of the challenges related to being a single woman raising five children. Mom, you are a strength and an inspiration. God bless.*

# FOREWORD

Once Jordan decided that he wanted to play in the NFL, he understood how to write a recipe for success and then applied it to every facet of his life.

Yet when Jordan was little, we (the family) never thought he would get into the NFL. He was small and was always clowning. We had no idea which direction he would land in. Yeah, he and I played football on our knees in the house and made a pact to join the league, but he just didn't seem to take anything seriously. But then his senior year of high school, Jordan decided to push himself. The growth that resulted from that was staggering.

First, he joined me at Iowa to train for an entire summer. At the time, Jordan was at a Division ll school and knew that if he wanted to get into the NFL, he'd have to up his training game. Watching him at the Iowa practices, it was clear that Jordan had set his mind on the NFL. At that point, there was no stopping him.

In *Pivot to Win*, Jordan talks about the perseverance, grit, determination, and hard work that allowed him to beat odd after odd until and after he created a decade-long career in the NFL. I know how much I've learned from Jordan, which is why he's sharing the lessons he's learned with others. It doesn't matter if you're a doctor, lawyer, NFL player, entrepreneur, or college student, these are the characteristics of a successful life determined by a series of well-executed pivots. No matter what you do or who you are, we are all human and we can all learn from the humanity that Jordan shares in *Pivot to Win*.

Jonathan Babineaux, Jordan's older brother and former NFL defensive tackle, Atlanta Falcons

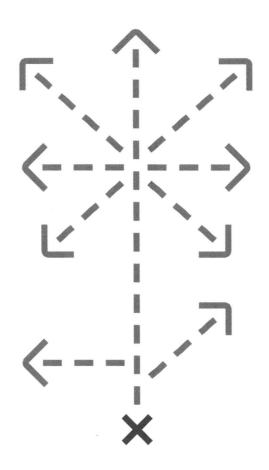

"It's not the strongest of the species that survives, nor is it the most intelligent … it is the one who is most adaptable to change."

—Charles Darwin

# INTRODUCTION

"Bring it in, guys," said Uncle Dwight, motioning for my brother Jonathan (Monsta) and me to bring our bikes to a halt along the seawall in Port Arthur, Texas. It was a typical sunny February day and the air smelled faintly of oil. Uncle Dwight took a knee and then reached for each of our hands. Uncle Dwight, who we called Godfather, was my father's youngest brother. He was one of those guys who are great with kids but doesn't have any of his own. Godfather was always at our house taking me and my four siblings on beach outings and camping trips, bringing us treats, and making sure we were minding Mama.

As Godfather took both of our hands, I took a deep breath, inhaling the chemical smell of the refineries that kept 80 percent of Port Arthur residents provided with food, water, and shelter. Monsta and I had spent the afternoon racing each other around the big boulders that anchored the shores of the Sabine-Neches Waterway.

"I'm sorry to tell you boys this," Godfather said, "but your father has passed away."

Passed away? I looked at Godfather, utterly confused. At eight years old, I understood that death meant that someone wasn't coming back, but I didn't understand death or what it would mean for Monsta and me—let alone my whole family. After Godfather told us that my dad had died, I don't remember how we got back to the house or what Mama said to us. I do remember feeling a heavy sense of loss, an emptiness as if someone blew a hole through my chest.

My father, Joseph "Butch" Babineaux, died in a freak accident on February 8, 1991. A Vietnam veteran, my dad was at a local vet hospital for a general checkup. While he was waiting for the doctor, he stepped out of the waiting room on the fourth floor, lit a cigarette, leaned against a loose balcony, and fell to his death.

Almost overnight, Mom started worrying about bills, how she would pay for college, and how she would keep her five kids on the right track. While she suffered and mourned, family and friends moved through our house shocked and grieving. I remember the house being our "safe place" but also feeling like I didn't belong there. Mama was so distraught that she could hardly contain herself. To temporarily relieve us from the trauma, we kids spent a few nights at my grandpa's house. While she was moving through her grief, Mama kept her job at Southwestern Bell and then added second jobs whenever she could, leaving each of us to essentially care for ourselves.

Monsta and I are eleven months apart in age, so wherever Monsta went, I went. Whatever Monsta wanted to do, I wanted to do, and whatever he did, I wanted to do better. Right after Dad's death, the one thing both of us wanted more than anything was to eliminate Mom's pain.

When Dad died, we moved back into his house, which is where we lived before my parents divorced. Boy, was that eerie! One night, sitting on our bedroom floor, Mom's wails rising in the background, Monsta and I made a pact: We would find jobs that would prevent Mom from ever having to worry about money again. Because we were naïve and didn't know that only 1.6 percent[1] of college football players actually make it to the National Football League (NFL), we decided that we'd become NFL players.

We didn't know anything about the NFL other than what we saw on TV. To us, the NFL was a bunch of seriously strong dudes making courageous tackles and spiking footballs into the end zone after driving past the defense for game-winning touchdowns. We knew those guys couldn't possibly worry about money, not with the flashy jewelry, houses, and cars

1 http://www.ncaa.org/about/resources/research/football-probability-competing-beyond-high-school

they had. They looked healthy, they looked happy, they were rich—and we wanted a piece of what they had. Without any question, the NFL was going to be our ticket out of Port Arthur.

Like music artist Janis Joplin, Pro Football Hall of Fame Coach Jimmy Johnson, hip-hop duo Underground Kingz, NBA champion Stephen Jackson, and NFL player Tim McKyer, we were going to put Port Arthur on the map. Many people consider the southeast part of the state the "armpit of Texas," due to the heavy oil production. With Beaumont and Orange as neighboring cities to Port Arthur, at one time the area produced more pro football players and Super Bowl champions than anywhere else in the country. Aaron Brown, who attended my high school, played in the first AFL-NFL World Championship Game.

So we got to work. We joined the peewee football teams and, when Mom wasn't home, we tackled each other until the walls shook. Mom didn't say much about our dream. She was just happy that, while she was working, two of her kids were on the football field staying out of trouble. For Monsta and me, trouble meant more than it might have for the white kids. There was a time when every Black mother living on the west side of Port Arthur had warned their sons and daughters not to slip up and "accidentally" cross into the white side of town.

Growing up in the South, we experienced racism, but as kids we weren't able to synthesize it well enough to know the depth of those prejudices. It wasn't until I got older and had my own experiences that I realized the severity of generational discrimination. In our city of Port Arthur and in surrounding areas, the KKK not only was visible but also threatened Black people with intimidation, violence, and murder. Less than a fifteen-minute car ride from the house we grew up in, a billboard on the highway displayed a version of the following: "N*****, don't let the sun set on you here." This was the early 1990s when we would play little league football games and pack half the town to travel with us for safety. We'd blow out our white adversaries and have to run straight to the bus when the clock hit zero to get out as fast as we could. Anything could happen—the referees were known to make fake calls, our competitors would take cheap hits, we were even chased off of football fields for whooping up on the white teams. Things had gotten so bad by the time we got to high school that just miles away—in the same areas we used to avoid as kids—three white men tied a Black man to the tail of a pickup truck and dragged him to his death.

Kids who grew up in Port Arthur had two options: Graduate from high school and work for the refinery for about $70,000 or fall victim to the street life. Some went off to college, left, and never came back, but only a few. The choice between drugs and life was the first major decision every kid in my neighborhood made—but Monsta and I, we made a third choice. That choice was sports. For Monsta and me, it started in our house. Our older brothers set the pace for sports. Then each of my siblings was accepted into college, and we both knew that the expectation was higher education.

I was a star in little league football, but by the time I got to high school, it felt like I had to work extra hard to get playing time. There were a lot of talented kids from the neighborhood and we all wanted a way out. I was undersized and fast, but no matter what I did I was always the underdog. In college, I had to fight to earn a scholarship. In the NFL, I had to fight to get exposure to as many teams as possible. Then I had to fight to get on the roster—and then I had to fight to stay on the roster. But I've never been afraid of the fight. I love the fight. I love breaking down barriers and testing what I'm made of. I love putting my finger on something, saying, "I'm going to do this, and dammit, I'll do it just because you said I couldn't!"

Coming out of high school, I was lucky to play for Division II Southern Arkansas University as a defensive back. It didn't take long to see playing time. Going into my senior year of college, no one expected to see anything more from me as a football player. They thought I would finish the season playing the way I had my sophomore and junior years, since playing at the next level is a rare feat. No one expected to hear from me again. No one except for me.

See, what other people didn't know is that between my junior and senior year, I met with a man who was also an NFL football scout. I asked him to lunch and when we sat down, I said, "How do I get to the NFL?" He said, "You need to get bigger and I want you to return kicks."

Not long after that conversation, I was on the road to Iowa to train with Monsta at the University of Iowa, a Division I school that had a topnotch football program led by coach Kirk Ferentz. That entire summer,

I worked just as hard as everyone on Monsta's team, sometimes harder. I trained, made a point to be the first one in and the last one gone, and slept on Monsta's couch. Then I woke up and did it all over again.

By the end of the summer, I left Iowa City exuberant and confident. I increased my weight and speed and returned to Southern Arkansas demanding a cornerback position and a special teams assignment. In 2003, which was my senior year, I earned NCAA All-America First-Team honors as a cornerback and kick returner. I also received NCAA All-Region First-Team and All-GSC First-Team honors as a cornerback. I had sixty-eight tackles (forty unassisted), defended fourteen passes, recovered three fumbles, picked off five passes, and earned a trip to the Whataburger Cactus Bowl, the Division II All-Star game in Kingsville, Texas. I also caught the attention of both the Tampa Bay Buccaneers and the Detroit Lions, which felt pretty damn good.

By the time the 2004 draft rolled around, both the Bucs and the Lions had lost interest in me. However, I was confident that I could play at the next level if I got an invite to any team's training camp. Day three of the NFL draft, I got a call from a Seattle area code and when I answered, the voice of defensive coordinator Ray Rhodes offered me a position with the Seahawks. I could hardly contain my excitement. I kept thinking, "Hell, yeah!"

With all the odds stacked against me, I walked onto the Seahawks field as an undrafted free agent and started showing my team why I belonged. For the next seven years, I persisted, I trained, I grew, I dug deep, I worked hard, and I performed until the only place for me on the Hawks roster was a starter position. During that time, I also suffered injuries, helped bring the Hawks to Super Bowl XL, went through a difficult coaching turnover twice, dealt with the harsh reality of the business of football, and joined the Tennessee Titans. But what I really did, just like my brother, was join the ranks of the nobodies who crawled out of Port Arthur and gave hope to young players looking to fulfill their own NFL dreams—people like Jamaal Charles, Kevin Everett, Danny Gorrer, and two-time Super Bowl champ Elandon Roberts.

For many people, having an NFL career of any length would be a marker of success, a good place to stop and say, "Hey, look what I did." Not for me. The NFL is just one chapter in the Jordan Babineaux playbook. Playing in the NFL is just one challenge that needed discipline and a plan for overcoming obstacles. When that chapter closed after the 2012 season, I knew I needed to start looking for the next chapter. It was time to pivot.

If you're a football fan, you may have read a few stories about ex-NFL players who have struggled to transition out of the NFL. It's understandable. The NFL is not like ordinary life. It's a very extravagant lifestyle where everything is five stars, gourmet chefs are at your fingertips, and anything and everything that you could want at a moment's notice is accessible. Getting away from this and then using that NFL chapter as a stepping-stone to an even greater chapter is difficult for most players.

When I retired from the NFL in 2012, I knew I was facing a startling statistic: Seventy-eight percent of NFL players are bankrupt or under financial stress within two years of leaving the league.[2] I did not want that for myself or my family, so I planned for failure. Several years before I left the NFL, I started investing in my future. First, I put my broadcast journalism degree to work by starting a couple of radio shows. Then, in 2010, two years before I retired, Monsta and I started a production company called 2 Brothers. In between those two successes, there were a few failed investment attempts and a tuition cost attributed to pivoting through the School of Life. I'll talk about those lessons throughout the book.

Today, just like when I was in the NFL or when I was training at Southern Arkansas, what stands in the way of what we desire is what we do every day. Goals can be achieved with the effort of consistent practice. If you fall short, the journey is well worth the attempt. It is the person we become that makes setting goals worth it. It's the reason I am sharing this book as well as my experiences, successes, failures, and lessons about what I did well and could have done better. I squandered away hundreds of thousands of dollars in a sickness of impulsive spending, started businesses that failed, and nearly went bankrupt trying to maintain a certain lifestyle. On the flipside, I've also started companies that provide economic stability, given thousands of dollars to charitable causes, and helped others achieve their mission on their journey.

In *Pivot to Win*, I'm going to show you how to bring a dream to fruition, how to leverage your skills to reinvent yourself (or your company), and how to recognize when it's time to pivot. I'm going to show

2 https://fivethirtyeight.com/features/theres-a-difference-between-broke-and-bankrupt-for-ex-nfl-players/

you how to use your strengths and your adversities. I'm going to show you how to develop a growth mindset. I'll show you how to take the lessons you learn in this book and apply them to your business or your professional life.

At the end of this book, you will:

→ Know how to **leverage** your odds to maximize your winning potential.
→ Recognize your **pivot** so that you can move from being stuck toward success, achievement, and greater purpose.
→ **Transition** better when change happens.

We'll identify each of your assets so that when you're ready to play your game, you won't find yourself on the sidelines.

There isn't a single person in this world that lives one chapter their entire lives. Things happen—careers change, relationships end, crises happen, and the world grows in ways that might not benefit your current position. That's okay, because you can change too.

Whether you're a CEO, an athlete, a homemaker, a leader in your organization or family, or an entrepreneur, *Pivot to Win* is for you. The tools in this book are not just for NFL players; they're for any company that wants to grow new ways of serving customers and any individual who wants to evolve so that when change happens, you can accelerate into living your purpose.

When you're ready to take the journey, I'm ready to take it with you!

With appreciation,

*Jordan Babineaux*

Jordan Babineaux

# SECTION 1
# Leverage Your Odds

Have you ever heard anyone complain about not achieving something because they didn't have access to the right person? Or maybe they were born in the wrong era. Or maybe they didn't have enough money, come from the right family, or have the right background.

It's time to say goodbye to that kind of thinking. Everybody has access. We live in a time where information is accessible with the click of a button. Even our cell phones offer a virtual assistant who stands at attention when it hears your voice. Access doesn't come from where you're born or who you know. It comes from within. It comes from sitting down with yourself, deciding what you want from your own life, and then taking steps to achieve your own goals. Build, work, dream, create. You are your own access.

Leveraging something means shifting momentum to achieve the results you desire. You can create your own access by leveraging the things that you have and the things that you don't. None of us were born in the same house, to the same parents, under the same circumstance, at the exact same second as someone else. Each of us has our own background, our own experience, our own strengths, and our own weaknesses. Each of us has advantages—sometimes disguised as disadvantages—that, given the right attitude, can make us unstoppable.

In Leverage Your Odds, I'll show you how I learned to leverage four specific qualities to achieve my first big goal: Playing in the NFL. These qualities include:

→ Adversity
→ Decision-making
→ Competition
→ Understanding my own mindset

On paper, as a small kid coming out of Port Arthur, Texas, without any access to the NFL, I shouldn't have ended up playing in the NFL, but I did. I shouldn't have ended up on the starting roster in the NFL, but I did. I certainly shouldn't have ended up playing in the Super Bowl—but I did.

Whether your dream is to play for a professional sports team, start a company, or become a better version of yourself, you can leverage each of your experiences to do just that. I will walk with you on this journey, but you have total control over how far we go together. At the end of each chapter, take some time to digest the material and consider how you can implement it in your life. I want you to think about the following questions. Really think about them. Jot down your thoughts, and then return to them after we finish this section.

When was the last time you used leverage—your skill set, relationships, or position—to help you achieve a specific outcome?

Looking back on a previous goal, did you use leverage? If not, could it have helped you?

What are you doing now where you can use leverage to help achieve your current goal?

Which three people can you call on to help you use leverage and gain momentum?

Are you ready? Okay, Coach just called the play!

Ready, set, go!

----------------------------------

"Refuse to believe any
circumstances sufficiently
strong enough to defeat
you in the accomplishment
of your purpose."

----------------------------------

—Earl Nightingale

# CHAPTER 1

# SOUTHERN ROOTS

I come from Port Arthur, Texas, home to some of the most resilient people I know. The town sits ninety miles east of Houston, bordering the Gulf of Mexico and the Louisiana state line. Port Arthur carries the identity of the entire state because it's known for oil and football. Friday night high school football—or, as we call it, "Friday night lights"—was epic.

I imagine that you've never been to Port Arthur. It's not a place that people go for vacation. It's a downtrodden, highly polluted, industrialized region, known mainly for the Keystone Pipeline, an oil pipeline system that runs to Canada. This is, in part, why the city suffers from social and economic downturn. Refineries produce over half a million barrels of oil daily, yet the city that supports the refinery is left in ruins from no reinvestment into the local community and the people within it.

Port Arthur is not a pretty place and it's not a place of high expectations. When I was growing up, two things were predicted for Port Arthur kids: Get swept up in the adversity of living in an environment of poverty and resort to selling drugs while trying not to get busted by the police . . . or get a job. There are thousands of small cities that resemble Port Arthur and its residents—Black kids who grow up in poverty, live in single-parent households, and have witnessed drug abuse and violence. We were at war with our circumstance and our future.

I didn't want to live my life either of the ways that Port Arthur offered. I followed in the footsteps of my older brothers and chose a third option. I decided to join the ranks of ballers who had already put Port Arthur on the map for something else: sports.

I was able to break away from conforming to that negative paradigm for two reasons. First, my mother kept us rooted in spirituality. God was nonnegotiable in our house. Second, I have always believed that the world was waiting for me to explore. There are ways to liberate yourself from any environment, any relationship, any way of thinking. As a kid, I lived in poor conditions, but I kept my imagination free to escape those conditions whenever I wanted. I do that to this day.

## DON'T ROLL OVER; JUMP OVER

I guess you could say I faced a lot of adversity when I was younger, but I never saw it that way. I saw it as, hey, this is my life. Things happen. It's your perspective, attitude, and actions that determine whether those things are good or bad.

- - - - - - - - - - - - - - - - - - - - - - - - - - - - - - - - - - - - - -

Things happen. It's your perspective, attitude, and actions that determine whether those things are good or bad.

- - - - - - - - - - - - - - - - - - - - - - - - - - - - - - - - - - - - - -

After my dad died when I was eight, I wouldn't say things got bad—I'd say that things got more challenging. Even though Mom was working three jobs and we had Dad's Social Security to help out, she still had six mouths to feed and only one of them was making money. But there are people who complain about tough circumstances holding them back and there are people who embrace them. In Mama's house, there was no complaining. No matter what adversity we face, you embrace it, learn how to make the best of it, and move on. This is how Monsta and I became chefs before we were ten years old. At the end of the month, when the cabinets were bare, Monsta and I got creative with two of the cheapest ingredients we could—rice and bread. We put anything we could on bread and we mixed anything we could with rice. This game of bread and rice didn't make us feel bad or less-than; it made us use our imaginations. Cheese toast was a meal. So was a syrup sandwich and eggs and rice.

By the time middle school rolled around, we were used to the changes in our family. We knew money was tight, but we didn't let that stop us. I don't know if you remember what it's like to be in middle school with everyone always looking around to see what everyone else is wearing, but in the '90s, the thing everyone wanted to own was one of those Will Smith "Fresh Prince of Bel-Air" silk button-up shirts and a fresh pair of Air Jordans. I had one of those shirts, but it was from my oldest brother, Jeff, so I swam in it. Hand-me-downs happened quite a bit in my family. As the youngest, I always got my big brothers' clothes. I don't remember if anyone said anything about it, but that's because if they did, I wouldn't have let it bother me.

The other issue with my gear was that I started middle school wearing last year's shoes. The school year always starts with new stuff—new school supplies, new clothes, new shoes—but Mom couldn't afford new. When she said, "You're wearing last year's shoes," that was that, case closed. What's on your feet says a lot about your swag. When I started the seventh grade with last year's kicks, I did all I could to wash the shoestrings and used shoe polish to make them look fresher.

I went to school in a too-big silk shirt and last year's shoes, and I got through it because I decided not to make a thing about it. Thank goodness baggy clothes were in style! I decided not to let something that was out of my control define who I wanted to be in life or at school. If wearing the coolest, newest gear was going to be the obstacle, I was going to jump right over it and never look back. If you asked me about my style then, I would have told you that I was the best dressed.

The best thing about this story is that, looking forward ten years, I would be getting a new pair of shoes every week. Not only that, but also I didn't pay a single cent for them. Who would've thought making it to the NFL would warrant all the gloves, shoes, wristbands, and apparel a person needed? As part of our contracts, sports apparel companies make sure equipment is accessible. If I had let the adversity of poverty roll me over, I never would have jumped out of those old shoes into new shoes.

When you're given the choice to roll over or jump over—old shoes, new shoes, no shoes—get to jumping!

---

When you're given the choice to roll over or jump over—old shoes, new shoes, no shoes— get to jumping!

---

## DO YOU WANT TO PLAY OR NOT?

Before Monsta and I played any sort of little league football, we crushed game after game of knee ball in our living room. When Mom wasn't home, we'd play tackle football in the house, but on our knees. We'd take shoulder pads out of Mama's blazers (remember, this is the early '90s) to make our own gear. Then we'd roll up about twenty socks to make a football and get to work tossing each other all over the living room. It's no surprise that when Coach Snowden saw us horsing around in the local grocery store, Mom viewed his intervention in our lives as divine.

After we came close to knocking over one of those end displays of stacked boxes, Coach Snowden approached Mom and said, "You should put these boys in Pop Warner" (it's the same as little league football). It didn't take but a second for Mom to see what a good idea it would be to redirect our energy, so she scraped together enough money to pay the registration fee and we started playing football.

Man, was that an exciting time for us! Not only did we get to play football, but we got to dress like actual football players. Mom took us to a local sports shop to get our gear. Before we got there, I envisioned myself rocking the legendary Hall of Famer Emmitt Smith's birdcage helmet—you know, that tight helmet that all skill players were wearing in the 1990s. When we arrived, I told the clerk exactly what I wanted. As he took us past other useful gear like shoulder pads and pads for our pants, I ignored every suggestion he made until we reached the helmets. When I saw the birdcage gleaming from its stand, I said, "That's my helmet! That's it right there! Can I try it on?"

"Sir," Mom said, "how much is that helmet?"

Whatever that man said was too much because, before I could get that helmet on my head, Mom grabbed my upper arm and pulled me back from the mirror. Then she pushed that helmet so far up on that shelf that I didn't think anyone would ever see it again. The only helmet Mom could afford that season was a kicker's helmet. Compared to Emmitt Smith's birdcage, the kicker's helmet was the ugliest, lowest-profile helmet out there. If you don't believe me, search the internet for kicker Morten Andersen. Morten Andersen came into the NFL in 1982, the year I was born, and finished his career as my brother's teammate in Atlanta.

Andersen may have kicked his way into Canton, Ohio, as a member of the Pro Football Hall of Fame, but an eight-year-old kid saw nothing exciting about a kicker's helmet. The birdcage had a protective face mask with multiple bars. This helmet was wide open in the front. I believed that any single hit would break my entire face. It was clearly designed for someone who wasn't planning on seeing a whole lot of action. Any kid who played football or watched the NFL knew what Emmitt Smith's helmet looked like just like they knew what a kicker's helmet looked like—and I wasn't out there to be a kicker. But when your family doesn't have money, and the option is looking like Morten Andersen or not playing, you accept it. I figured there was no point in asking for the visor. "Thank you, sir."

My hatred for that helmet knew no bounds, but growing up with Mama, I knew that complaining wasn't an option. If I did, I knew that she would whip the car around and get her money back. So I wrapped my head around that kicker's helmet before we got home. By the time we reached the driveway, I thought, Hey, at least I get to play. Anything is better than playing knee ball with Monsta. And it was.

I had a flashback to this childhood moment when I got to rookie mini-camp with the Seahawks. In my locker hung an NFL jersey with Jordan Babineaux on it. I smiled as I touched the stitching of my last name. Even though it was number 43, I was happy to have a jersey. I noticed a note in my locker that read, "Helmet fitting in the equipment room."

I made my way through the double doors to the helmet fitting room. "I'm Babineaux, here for my helmet," I announced to the equipment manager. Directing my attention to the display behind him, he said, "Great. What style facemask do you like?"

I looked up at the wall of different helmets and facemasks, feeling like I had won a carnival game and it was time to select the grand prize. I scanned the options and, with a big smile, pointed to the famous birdcage.

One of the coolest things about being part of a professional sports franchise is that in less than five minutes, with a power drill and a few small screws, I had a newly assembled helmet. I tried it on and strapped my chinstrap for a final safety check. "Not too tight? Ears feel okay? Can you see clearly?" the equipment manager asked. "Yep," I confirmed. As I was leaving, he called out, "Good luck, stay healthy."

Most kids wouldn't think about receiving in those terms, but embracing that helmet as a child was an early lesson to practice control and acceptance that has served me well.I tried to assert my influence over the helmet, but it didn't work because I didn't actually have control over what type of helmet I could get—Mom did. After my influence fell flat, I accepted the reality of the situation. I wanted to play football, I needed a helmet to play football, my only option for a helmet was a kicker's helmet, so that's what I would wear to play. Case closed.

## WHY HAVING FAITH IN SOMETHING GREATER THAN YOURSELF MATTERS

One of the reasons that I became conditioned to accept things that I had little control over is that I was taught from a young age to have faith. Having faith can mean believing in God, a higher power, or another sense of spirituality, or it can mean having faith in yourself. For me, it means both.

We all have personal beliefs on religion, laws, and politics, but faith has impacted me too much for me to write a whole book without saying a thing about it. I grew up as a good old Catholic boy in the parish of the Sacred Heart Catholic Church, which was just steps away from Lincoln High School and down the street from my house. Sacred Heart was, and still is, old-school Catholic. You got a pinch in the pew from whatever church elder was closest if you wiggled too much. I sometimes attended the church of my friend, who grew up Baptist. Southern Baptist church service meant long days.

When I say that I grew up in the church, I mean that I was at Sacred Heart every single Sunday come rain, shine, or any excuse that I could possibly think of for not getting my butt in that pew. Even when Monsta and I got to high school and were able to drive, Mama didn't care if we were tired from hanging out too late the night before. She didn't care if it was a beautiful day and all that was on my mind was shooting hoops with friends or watching NFL games. Church was church, God was our savior, and my siblings and I were expected to respect and participate in that tradition every single Sunday.

Each of my siblings participated in church activities. I sang in the church and school choirs. In those days if you had a solo, you were a big deal, and I was one of the kids who had a solo. My choir teachers, Mr. Linden and Mrs. Green, parented us too, which is part of growing up in a small community. When I wasn't at school or playing sports, I participated in church outings—fundraisers, barbecues, bake sales, you name it. Every weekend we were out in the community raising money to attend national conferences. If I had been given the choice to do something—anything—other than going to church, I would have done the other thing. But then something happened (a pivot) that changed my life and provided a foundation for spiritual growth.

In junior high, I attended one of the many youth conferences that we spent weekends raising money to attend. For a span of three days, hundreds of youths in the state of Texas attended workshops on faith practices and life skills. I left the conference with a feeling of incredible power that I can only attribute to a higher power. I don't know why it happened then. Perhaps it was my dad's spirit, but it connected me to God. I don't know whether something was different with me or if it was something external, but that jump started a spiritual walk that has helped me throughout my adult life. Even today, when I am struggling or facing challenges, I resort to my spiritual foundation to find inner peace and calm. When you have faith in something greater than yourself, it's easy to not sweat the small stuff. It's easier to let things go.

---

When you have faith in something greater than
yourself, it's easy to not sweat the small stuff.
It's easier to let things go.

---

For me, having a strong faith in God makes it crystal clear that life
is not about the grind. It's about alignment. When alignment happens,
when everything is in balance, you'll experience that same sense of calm
that I first experienced when I was at that youth conference in Houston.
Spirituality is the centerpiece of peace.

## HAVE FAITH IN YOURSELF

I don't know why I always had faith in myself—maybe it was my early
experience at that youth conference and Mama keeping us in church—
but I had it. Growing up, I had this ability to sort of turn a blind eye to
adversity and make something positive out of it.

In middle school, Monsta and I became fixated with these strength
shoes that we saw in *Eastbay* catalog, the sports equipment magazine
that all the kids were passing around back in the day. There we'd see
the best sports gear anyone could find. When strength shoes came out,
every kid in Port Arthur wanted a pair. Strength shoes have this circu-
lar gadget under the toe part that attaches beneath the front of the shoe
so that when you put the shoe on, your heel doesn't touch the ground.
This causes whoever's wearing the shoe to walk on their tiptoes, thereby
strengthening their calves and lower legs throughout the day.

I wanted big calves and was sold on these shoes. If you used them to
train, the promise was that you'd get big calves and increase your vertical.
By high school, everyone wanted to dunk on a regulation basketball goal.
I thought, If I'm gonna jump ten feet to dunk, I need to get these shoes.
I wanted to dunk!

As cool as strength shoes were, we couldn't afford them. One day, I was
walking home and I saw my brother Jeff cut down a wood block and then
place it under the footpad of his tennis shoes using duct tape. He made
his own strength shoes! We were pretty damn creative. So I got out a
handsaw and made my own strength shoes. Those homemade shoes were

embarrassing and I never wore them in public. But quietly, I believed they would work. By the end of my tenth-grade year, I could dunk a basketball.

## DEFINE YOURSELF BEFORE ADVERSITY DOES

Growing up in Port Arthur, I was never told anything about adversity. I wasn't programmed to think that I couldn't do something or achieve something because the odds were stacked against me. We probably saw more things as a kid than Mama could control, but we never allowed our circumstances to define us.

I distinctly remember sitting in my high school class while the teacher, who was also my aunt Pie, said, "If you graduate high school, you'll make between this and this," as she pointed to two figures on the projector. "If you graduate from college, you'll make this amount." Here she referenced two numbers slightly higher than the previous ones. I didn't find it odd she was looking at me when she said this. It was clear graduating college was a goal. While my older siblings had already demonstrated that we could go to college, I knew that I would go to college the minute that I saw that statistic. I defined what I wanted for my life before I really even started living it.

Regardless of the adversity that you're going through, facing it means taking what you already have and making it work to your advantage. I saw Port Arthur as a magical place capable of producing some of this country's greatest musicians and athletes. It did. Troubles were present, but conflict is everywhere. I wasn't any luckier than any other kid who redeems the joy life offers. I saw the dangers of late-night hangouts and drug deals. I even participated in both, as you'll see in the next chapter, and it nearly jeopardized everything I had worked to achieve.

# ✕----------- PIVOT TO WIN -----------
# CHAPTER 1 RECAP

If there's one thing all of us can learn from adversity, it's that adversity makes us tougher and more resilient. When you leverage your own adversities, remember to:

**1) Embrace Struggle**
  Every day we face challenges, some big, some small. Think of a time when you have faced a challenge or adversity head-on. Now think of a time when you didn't. How did you feel after each situation? How would you act differently if you faced a challenge today?

**2) Have a Little Faith**
  I know that it's not in everyone's nature to have faith in something greater than themselves, but no matter who you are, you have to have faith in something. Otherwise, what's the point? At the very least, have faith in yourself.

**3) Find Your Own Strengths**
  Self-identity is powerful. Find your own strengths for yourself, not for other people. Talk to yourself like you're talking to your best friend. How do you describe yourself? What strengths do you list? What would your best friend, mother, or anyone else who supports and loves you add to that list?

>

"You cannot solve
a problem with
the same thinking
that created it."

— Albert Einstein

# CHAPTER 2

# A COSTLY FUMBLE

efining yourself means making decisions that align with who you want to become, not the stereotypes or adversities that have tried to take that power from you.

In my early twenties, I had overcome the odds of playing in the NFL. I was never the highest-paid player on the roster, but it was a pretty good lifestyle. If there was something I wanted and I didn't have it, I'd go get it. I guess you could say that it went to my head. If there is such a thing, I was a humble asshole. Midway through my career, I nearly lost it all when I made a terrible decision. It was the off-season, I had just finished visiting home, and I was leaving Houston to go back to Seattle.

As I got closer to the gate assigned to me by the airline, I got a funny feeling. I felt like I was being watched. Finally, I realized that two cops were walking from the gate toward me. That's when the source of that funny feeling clicked. Shit, I thought. I have cannabis in my checked bag.

At that time, cannabis was a coping mechanism for dealing with the pressure of a performance-based industry like professional sports. After multiple surgeries, I used it as a pain management treatment. Not thinking (obviously), I had thrown the cannabis into my bag as I scrambled to make the last nonstop flight from Bush International to SeaTac.

I slowly turned away from the gate, took out my phone to call my brother Josh, and continued walking as casually as I could while dialing. Josh is my second-oldest brother and lives in Houston. He's the sophisticated one. At least, that's what he thinks. When he got on the phone, I let him know that I thought I was about to be busted for carrying cannabis. We immediately started trying to figure out what might happen. What would the cops do? Would the NFL find out? Would I have to go to court? How would my mama react? It's amazing how quickly it becomes obvious that the potential consequences of a poorly made decision can affect every aspect of your life.

Although I thought I looked like your average guy just talking on the phone before a flight, the cops knew who they were looking for. They approached me, asked to see my ID, and demanded that I join them in a private room. Thankfully, there weren't any handcuffs or drama. I just had to walk through the airport looking pleasant with two police escorts in tow.

When we got to the room, they brought out my checked bag and asked me if it was mine. It felt like the longest one-second stare to the sound of "yes"—and the longest gulp of "oh, shit." Then the men pulled out a small bag of marijuana. They told me what was going to happen from that point forward, but I don't remember a single word they said.

We ended up at the downtown Houston station, where the cops took my mug shot and put me in a holding cell. I can tell you; a jail cell isn't the place for any VIP treatment. That was a fast goodbye to whatever lifestyle I had been living. It was a low point. I was smart enough to escape the prison traps in my neighborhood when I was a kid, but now I'm in the NFL and sitting behind bars? Hell no.

My brother was finally able to bail me out. I immediately called the team. I didn't know how much information they had, but the NFL has global contacts in law enforcement so my name could have generated an alert. Plus, I wanted to make sure I got ahead of the media before I became the latest dumbass to appear on the sports news ticker. Eventually I did become that person, but I owned my shit. As you can imagine, it didn't go well. I ended up in the office with the general manager, and awaited suspension from the NFL. Publicity is one of the benefits and downsides to being in the NFL—everything we do is under the microscope. It was a terrible decision that was driven by a feeling of invincibility and was one that jeopardized my entire future. When I sat in that jail cell unsure of the consequences, I realized that by making one stupid decision, I had completely let go of all control that I had over my future.

---

> ## When I sat in that jail cell unsure of the consequences, I realized that by making one stupid decision, I had completely let go of all control that I had over my future.

---

One of the consequences related to this choice was treatment. I had to go to therapy for thirty months. Through that process, I took a close look at self-identification and the environment of my upbringing. I took a long, hard look at what I thought was acceptable based on some of the life experiences that I had. I was horribly embarrassed about the situation and knew that, to ensure that I wouldn't do something like that again, I had to pivot from old ways of thinking and find alternative ways to ease the stresses of playing in the NFL and managing pain. It meant I had to change my habits.

Charles Duhigg identifies this as the Habit Loop in *The Power of Habit*. This means reprogramming your thought process to change your outcomes. This was an overnight decision for me once I was issued a suspension and put on probation by the league. When backed into a corner, I had the mental strength to flip the switch.

For me, part of this reprogramming was a game of trust. How do you trust yourself to make decisions after something like that? It's easy to say, "I won't do that again"—but what do you do when no one's watching? To regain trust in my own decisions, I had to re-learn self-accountability. Our choices become our habits. As with the good habits—putting in extra work, staying late, and studying the game of football—I had success. It was the questionable decisions that I had to hold myself accountable for. I used the time in therapy to talk through childhood experiences and leverage counseling to pivot to better decision-making.

# MAKE THE GOOD DECISIONS BY AVOIDING THE BAD

What do you do to keep your kids, who grow up in neighborhoods of crime, violence, and drug deals, out of trouble? How does a mother keep her African American boys safe from streets, jails, and police profiling and misconduct so that they return safely home to her? Mom's answer was to fill every free minute that Monsta and I had with some sort of activity. We went to school, we went to church, and we played every sport and participated in every extracurricular activity possible. By the time I got to junior high, I was already playing basketball, golf, and football. I was in the band, the choir, and whatever sporting season it was, that's what I played. I didn't even like track, but it was there and so I participated in it.

For the majority of school, I was a nerd. School came easy to me because learning was fun. When I finished my work earlier than other kids, I would bother them. I'd throw spitballs or play drums on my desk with my pencils because I was bored. Being the smart and bad kid in school was a combo that could have put me on a fast track to self-destruction. Instead, my energy was channeled into an area where I had the continuous ability to improve: sports. I loved that about sports, all sports. To this day, I still golf, which is a sport that I played in high school. Golf is like the journey I'm on—the journey that I hope you and I can take together—which is the road to be better. One day, I can score in the seventies. Other days, I fight to break ninety. It's like there's always something to work on and improve upon. In life, there's always something to learn, pursue, and improve upon too.

For me, and for many kids, playing sports is a vehicle that allows parents to shift bad energy into a better direction. My mom knew this. Sports taught me great life lessons about responsibility, commitment, and toughness even when it's hard. It pushes you to your breaking point and forces you to build courage and mental grit. For that, I've got my mom to thank. She's the reason that I started playing sports.

- - - - - - - - - - - - - - - - - - - - - - - - - - - - - - - - - - - - - - -

Sports taught me great life lessons about responsibility, commitment, and toughness even when it's hard.

- - - - - - - - - - - - - - - - - - - - - - - - - - - - - - - - - - - - - - -

In addition to putting my energy behind basketball, football, and golf, I excelled in school and was put into the academic program called Summit. Summit was a program that put academically advanced kids on a fast track of sorts. The curriculum was accelerated and we did different activities such as working with computers. Today, students work with computers when they're only two years old, but in the early '90s when computers were still in their infancy, few classrooms were equipped with online systems. We got to take really interesting classes like archery and swimming. We had to show that we valued education and then prove it by continually passing tests and excelling at other metrics to stay in the program.

Thanks to Summit, by the time I was in high school, I was programming BASIC and C++ code and thought that computer science was my calling. Both programming methods encompassed early stages of computer systems. I originally got into coding because I loved playing video games. I had gotten good enough at video games that I could beat many of them, but I had a crazy infatuation with what made my character jump, kick, or pick up a weapon based on one click of a button. For one of my high school projects, I created a hangman game for other students in my class to play.

By the summer before my senior year at Lincoln, I was so interested in coding that I went to Xavier University in New Orleans for six weeks to explore a program that showed me how to actually code. Both my brother Josh and my sister Jean attended Xavier. By this time, my three oldest siblings were attending historically Black colleges. I was sixteen years old playing mission-oriented video games, trying to pass each stage by figuring out the objectives, and learning how to make them at the same time.

Leaving New Orleans after being away from home for the first time, I was sure computer science was my journey. Sometime on the five-hour car ride home, I told my mother that I no longer wanted to play football so that I could spend more time focusing on coding and create my own video game. I'm not sure what she said about that decision, especially knowing that that season would be my last, but it was something like: "Don't you want to play one more year with your brother?" She left me to think about it. She was right. It was the last year and Monsta and I were on the same team. We led our school to the playoffs for the first time in over a decade and shared some great moments, so staying with the team was worth it.

# FIND PEOPLE WHO WILL HOLD YOU ACCOUNTABLE

I can still remember the march from my elementary school classrooms, through the courtyard, down the long concrete walkway to the school principal's office. Mr. Adams was a tall, dark-skinned bald man whose voice would tremble when he spoke—especially when he recounted whatever infraction of mine was on his mind that day. I told you I'd get bored and disturb my schoolmates. I would laugh so hard at clipping the heels of my classmates and causing other trouble that being the class clown was something that I lived up to.

Mr. Adams attended our church, so I had to see him not only during the week but also every Sunday. I surrendered everything that I did at school because when Mr. Adams saw Mom at church, I knew that, as soon as mass was over, he would tell her exactly what I had been up to. I had all the tricks—at least I thought I did. Because we walked to school, I would beat Mama home and erase messages from the answering machine that might implicate me in something. Mama don't play. If you embarrassed her, she was quick to discipline. So, every time she saw Mr. Adams at church, I would run home and do whatever I could to avoid my mom. Just when I thought I had pulled my best Houdini escape by spending all day out of the house, I'd get ready to slide into bed and find Mom waiting for me in the doorway, hands on hips.

Mom and Mr. Adams worked together to hold me accountable for every little thing. When I got to junior high, that baton was passed to Coach Getwood. "Coach G," as he was called, was an army vet, who was short and stocky and in his mid-forties. He was the school's disciplinarian for the football team. He lived near the projects with his son, who was older but always joined us for the neighborhood football game. Trust me, you had to be tough to play the way we did. Our boundaries for game time were between a fence and a street. Plenty of people ended up with scars from being tackled against the fence or the pavement.

Between Coach G, Mr. Adams, and my mom, there was no question as to whether I would toe the line. If Mom wasn't around because she was working, Coach G would step in. He didn't stand for bad grades, but that wasn't an issue for me. He didn't stand for fighting, stealing, or any BS— which sometimes got me in hot water.

As a kid, I didn't have any control over who decided to hold me accountable for my actions, but I'm sure glad that numerous people agreed to fill that role. Without them and without the maturity to hold myself accountable for my own decision-making, I have no idea what kind of decisions I might have made or how they might have affected my future.

## THIS INCLUDES YOU!

When you're a kid, hopefully you've got adults holding you responsible for your decisions and showing you how to correct or learn from poorly made ones. But what happens once you're an adult? Obviously when you play a team sport, your teammates, your coaches, and the fans hold you accountable. They don't let you get away with anything! But what happens when you're alone? What happens when you've made a decision that's landed you in a jail cell and no one else knows about it? That's when the only person you can look to for guidance is yourself. This is why, after my arrest, I worked so hard to get at the root of that decision, why I thought it was okay, and then determined that I would change that thought process so I would never end up in a similar situation.

While it's important to build a strong circle of accountability and influence around you, it's equally important to hold yourself accountable for your own actions. You're the one who is going to have to live with whatever decision you're making. When faced with a decision, make the decision your future self would be happy with. In this instance, I didn't do that, and it was a lesson to remember.

---

While it's important to build a strong circle of accountability and influence around you, it's equally important to hold yourself accountable for your own actions. You're the one who is going to have to live with whatever decision you're making.

---

## RUN WITH THE RIGHT CROWD

One hot, muggy summer day in Port Arthur, I was playing basketball with dozens of other junior high kids, pretending to be Michael Jordan. The asphalt was scalding hot, we knew most of the chain nets would be gone by Labor Day, and we could hear the neighborhood kids splashing and screaming away at the nearby community pool.

"Pass it, pass it!" a kid yelled. He didn't care that he wasn't open. He wanted the ball so that he could go one-on-one with the other team, score a bucket, and talk trash. That was his style. My style was that of a slasher, so I cut to the rim, received a pass from my teammate, and laid the ball in for the game-winning shot.

"Yeah, motherfucker!" I yelled with excitement. Those Port Arthur pickup courts were fierce and to hold your place, especially as a younger kid, was a big deal. So, after I scored, I just kept on shit-talking. For anyone unfamiliar with our style of play and celebration, it would have looked like a fight was about to break out, but I wasn't looking to fight anyone. I was looking to let everyone know that even though I was young, even though I'd left those courts bloody and bruised on dozens of occasions, I had just kicked some ass. I didn't even take a break as the next two teams got ready to take the court.

I didn't have to worry about a fight breaking out. I was headed for something worse. There I was just doing my thing. Finally, I stopped talking shit long enough to get a drink of water and lace up my shoes. As I stood up, my nose bumped up against the barrel of a six-shooter handgun. Oh shit, I thought. I'd heard about stuff like this happening in my neighborhood, but I had never been faced with it. I was an athlete and a Summit kid and in my own neighborhood, where it was understood that athletes were left alone. Everyone else in the neighborhood knew we weren't interested in getting involved in their shit because we were working toward something else.

"Hey man, what the fuck is wrong with you?" I courageously asked the kid holding the gun.

"You better stop talking so much shit," said this kid. I recognized him as one of the kids from the projects who was constantly getting picked on. This kid was scrawny and not that tough, but that day he was holding a pistol to my head. I tried to get that fool to relax. Before I could do or say anything, he took off running for home, but the experience left an impression. I may have appeared in control, but there's nothing about having the barrel of a gun in your face that's calming.

I'll never know if that gun was loaded, but I'll also never forget how it made me feel. There's no fear like the fear of staring down a gun barrel. That day, I thought my life was over. As much as I wanted to chase that fool down all the way to his house, I knew he had no respect for life. Not his or mine.

Although I continued playing ball the rest of that summer and many following, that incident was a reminder that the decisions I had made up until that point were the right ones. Despite seeing and playing with kids in my neighborhood, I never really knew most of them. That summer was a reminder that I needed to keep it that way. Years later, I found out that same kid spent significant time in and out of jail.

Parents, coaches, and other adults who try to protect us as kids only have control of us for so long. At some point, your decisions—good, bad, ugly—are yours. No excuses about being in the wrong place at the wrong time or hanging out with the wrong crew are valid. Still, despite how I've lived my life, I have to remind myself to hang with people who have high expectations. You are never too old to remember: "Bad company corrupts good character."[1]

---

> At some point, your decisions—good, bad, ugly—are yours.

---

## GOD WATCHES OVER BABIES AND FOOLS

My future was constantly under threat when I was a kid. I can think of several instances when one wrong decision, one minute too long in the wrong place, would've jeopardized my entire future. So how did I toe the line? Some of it was my mom, my coaches, and my mentors—and some of it was just pure luck.

---

1 *1 Cor 15:33*

Ever since we were in little league attending high school football games in our jerseys, we looked forward to high school. Playing football was nice and all, but our band was one of the best in the state of Texas. It was the high school version of what you'd see at an HBCU halftime "Battle of the Bands" performance. Choreographed dance moves to the sound of horns blaring, high-stepping drum majors, and a drum line that used difficult drumstick patterns to add style and pizzazz—it was something to see. Lincoln was the only high school on the west side of Port Arthur. It was the school for Blacks during the early years when segregation had a real presence. The pride of being a Bumblebee, our school's mascot, ran generations strong.

In school, many of my classmates took pride in getting good grades. High school academics was competitive. All the kids in Summit were in a battle to finish in the magna cum laude or cum laude percentile. Everyone wanted to stand out as the "smart kid." I graduated with honors—top 15 percent—which was something to celebrate. I went to a good school, I had a mom who cared, I had siblings to show me the way, and I had other people watching out for me.

I've noticed that people often chalk up the success of others to luck. When I was a kid, Mom had her own take on that. She was convinced that one of God's primary responsibilities was to look over babies and fools. Whether Mom is right or luck is a thing that some of us come across and some of us don't, I like what Oprah says about luck: "Luck is a matter of preparation meeting opportunity." Make the decisions in your work or personal life that best prepare you to meet opportunity.

- - - - - - - - - - - - - - - - - - - - - - - - - - - - - - - - - - - - -

> Make the decisions in your work or personal life that best prepare you to meet opportunity.

- - - - - - - - - - - - - - - - - - - - - - - - - - - - - - - - - - - - -

## SEE IT AND BELIEVE IT

My wife thinks I'm a hoarder because I keep stacks of magazines all over the place. She'll wait a few weeks and then she'll ask if she can clean them out, which is her way of warning me that she's ready to toss them in the recycling. It's funny because I never sign up to receive monthly publications but, somehow, I mysteriously get magazines in the mail. I am likely to use them for a specific reason: scanning the pictures in those magazines. They're full of ideas and inspiring stories from around the world that almost always trigger a new concept, design, or belief to discover new possibilities. I even rip out the pictures that I like when I want to make a new vision board. Capturing those images helps me embed the ideas in my head so that one day they can become my reality. I am a believer that expectation leads to manifestation.

Even before visualization and vision boards became a known thing to me, I was visualizing what I wanted for my future. As a kid, I imagined meeting people from all over the world and telling them about what it was like to grow up in Port Arthur. When I went to Xavier that summer in high school to learn how to code, that's exactly what I did. I met kids from all over the world and told them about my reality while also hearing different accents and learning about places that I'd never even heard of through stories told by other students.

Whether you plan to do it formally or informally, creating a vision of where you want to go is the only way you're going to get there. I know it might have sounded crazy when Monsta and I made a pact to get into the NFL. What little kid doesn't want to be a professional athlete? What little kid doesn't make a promise to do something great when they're an adult, especially for Mama? Sometimes the vision seemed clearer and more attainable than other times, but it was always there waiting for both of us to take the millions of little steps that we needed to get there. When you create a vision for yourself and you return to that vision daily, that vision becomes your reality. "We become what we think about,"[2] as Earl Nightingale reminds us in the "Strangest Secret" audio recording.

I didn't know what I was doing when I started visualizing the NFL for myself when I was a little kid, but it was neither the first nor the last time that I used visualization to sculpt something I wanted to do. My parents didn't graduate from college, but I saw myself in college classes, especially after all three of my older siblings went off to college. I saw myself graduating from college and I did exactly that. We all did. This is why

---

2 https://youtu.be/EFhkdzj-x8o

Mama is the reason for our success. She created a model for us to see so that we could visualize what we wanted for our lives. She showed us that you can do anything that you put your mind to, that spirituality and hard work are important, that being uncompromising in who you are and what you want is the only way to be. My siblings and I each graduated from high school and college, and my brother and I played over twenty years in the NFL combined. By envisioning what I wanted for my future, I was able to connect the actions needed to reach my goal.

## LEARN FROM YOUR MISTAKES

I've made lots of poor choices in my life, each of which I always self-examine. Bad choices have cost me friendships, time, and money. They've forced me to take longer, tougher paths to desired outcomes and they've caused me to take wrong turns, get bad breaks, and mismanage resources. From those lessons came breakthroughs. I've reestablished boundaries, deepened spirituality, and created a new vision for myself. It required me to accept my reality, identify things that matter most to me, and design a life where the legacy would outlive those early mishaps. The bad decisions that I've made and the circumstances that I've come from have never defined me. I hope the same is true for you.

# PIVOT TO WIN
# CHAPTER 2 RECAP

The only way to truly leverage your own life is to take responsibility for it. We are the accumulation of choices that we make. This is what I've learned about making choices:

### 1) Find People Who Will Hold you Accountable

I don't mean find people who support your bad habits. Find the ones who support your good habits and push you to develop new habits. Ask yourself, Who do I know who lives a life that I want to live? Who around me has a set of morals that I would like to mirror? Then interview those people. How do they live? How can you act in a similar way? What kinds of actions can the two of you take to hold each other accountable to your goals?

### 2) Visualize What You Want from Your Own Life

Find images that support that vision and put them up in your office or home. Envision acting as the person you want to become. Use images, audio, and words to reinforce what you want to do in life. The power of visualizing your path will help reinforce good decisions and minimize your chances of making mistakes.

### 3) Learn from Your Mistakes

Think about a choice that you've made that doesn't align with the person you want to become. What can you do to prevent yourself from being in that situation again? Who can you rely on to help you stay out of toxic environments? What do you need to change?

"It's not about what you're capable of, it's about what you're willing to do."

—Mike Tomlin

# CHAPTER 3

# A BIG BROTHER CHALLENGE

✕

t's 1995. Monsta and I have been working our tails off to make the top team at Woodrow Wilson Middle School. Woodrow Wilson was one of three middle schools in the city and everyone knew that if you wanted to play sports, you went to Woodrow. At Woodrow, the football players would run through brick walls just to prove their toughness. That's what it seemed like to me anyway, after spending the first few years of football in the little league. This wasn't the runt-weight class games where I uses to juke and outrun defenders to the end zone. These guys were BIG and intimidating, and they certainly didn't have any interest in losing their positions to younger, scrappier kids like me.

On the first day of tryouts, I stood on the sideline sizing up the other players. Despite ripping the little league circuit as one of the most skilled players on the field, that first day I felt a little bit out of my depth. As I scanned all of the middle schoolers, I looked for a favorable matchup by trying to rate each person who was standing in the blazing August heat with their hand-me-down high school equipment, huge thigh pads, and neck rolls. The linebackers and fullbacks stood to increase their stature and use the intimidation factor. The deep voice of what sounded like a military drill sergeant said, "Hey, kid, what position are you trying out for?" It was Coach G.

Startled, I turned around, straightened, and said, "Wide receiver."

"Then head down to the other end of the field, and no walking," Coach shouted.

That's when I noticed that every position used a certain part of the field as their warmup area. As I located the receivers, I began to jog. We hadn't even started practice, I was sweating like crazy, and I was out of my league. But I wanted to play, and I knew that to play, I had to compete. I had to learn about this new environment.

So I worked, hoping that if I put in enough time, I'd make the A team. The football program broke down into three teams. The A team was the best team and comprised mostly eighth graders and really good seventh graders, many of them much larger than any kid I'd ever seen outside of the field. The B team was usually a combination of good seventh graders and mediocre eighth graders, and the C team was for the not-so-good players, mostly seventh graders.

On the last day of tryouts, Monsta and I split ways while walking home. Monsta stopped at the store to get a snack, and I ran straight home to sit and wait by the phone. Coach said he'd call the players who made the A team. I desperately wanted to make that team. I didn't have to wait long before the phone started to ring. Sure enough, the caller ID said Woodrow Wilson Middle School.

"Hello?" I said after the first ring, sure that Coach G was about to tell me how great I was, how he couldn't wait to add me to the A team roster.

"Hey, Jordan, this is Coach G. Is Monsta there?"

Completely taken aback, I remembered my manners and told Coach Monsta wasn't there but that I could take a message. The silence was deafening and long. I knew that coach had some news to share, so I went out on a limb. "Coach," I said, "did I make the A team?"

"Actually, that's what I wanted to talk to Monsta about. He's on the A team. Practice is at 3:30. Can you make sure he gets the message?" Damn! Suddenly, I had become the messenger. Monsta and I competed in everything as kids. I was pissed off when he made the team and I didn't. I made sure he got the message, but I knew I had to do something to regain the edge in our competitive brother matchups.

## ALWAYS DO YOUR BEST

No matter the condition, circumstance, or obstacle, always give your best. That's how I've viewed competition my entire life. When I was young, my main competition was often Monsta. He and I were closer than my two older brothers, Jeff and Josh. They didn't let me hang around much. I was the pesky little brother. I feel like they had their own game of competition much like Monsta and I did. Jeff was the oldest and took no shortcuts on the big-brother headlocks, which was his way of making me tougher. Growing up with Monsta, I'd go back and forth with him in competitions. We did this in little league, we did this in high school, we did this in the NFL. Our whole lives have been a ping-pong game of who is better. We competed in everything—who is faster to the car to ride shotgun (front seat), who is the better football player, who is the better golfer.

We played one-on-one basketball games. We raced to see who could eat their food the fastest (I always won). Then one day, Monsta tricked me and changed the challenge to who could eat their food the slowest.

Monsta had good feet for a big guy. In the neighborhood basketball games, he'd dare to play point guard; but on the football field, he'd run your ass over. It pissed me off if he ever beat me in anything. I was faster, and more agile, and I could run like a deer. But he won a lot.

Monsta and I are as different as two brothers can be. Monsta is physically a lot bigger than me—that's why we call him Monsta. Because I was scrawny, I always played a level under Monsta throughout the early stages of football. Competitively, the biggest similarity between us is that neither of us will back down. Monsta doesn't want to lose to me, and I'm damn sure not losing to him.

Growing up with a competitor in the household not only helped me understand that you can always level up your game, but it also helped me appreciate other people's gifts and skills.

## NEVER LOSE YOUR BROTHER

In 2018, there were a total of twenty-nine sibling pairs in the NFL.[3] With roughly 1,696 players in the entire league, that means 3 percent of NFL players were siblings. Combined with the odds of a college football player being drafted by the NFL at 1.6 percent,[4] that says something about how the lifelong competition between Monsta and me helped both of us achieve a dream most siblings do not.

Monsta and I developed an early hunger for competition without even knowing it. We were brothers in life, but we were also brothers in competition. Our childhood was full of challenges. We would compete at anything—a foot race, a bike ride, who would end a football game with the most tackles, who could hit a stop sign with a rock from the farthest distance. Whatever we were doing, we were doing it to win.

## COMPETING WITH YOURSELF ISN'T ENOUGH

Competing with yourself is good. It helps fuel that internal fire to do better—but I experience moments when it's not enough. Anyone climbing to the top of their game can use an external motivator. The few times that I was able to play the Indianapolis Colts when Peyton Manning was the quarterback, we knew that he had seen every defense and knew how to attack it. We worked to disguise our coverage, with the defensive backs moving in sync at the snap of the ball to our positions so Manning wasn't playing "pitch and catch." Most of the time, he did anyway.

While looking outside for competition is good, be careful how you use it. If you use it to beat yourself up, it can have a negative effect—especially when you see others having faster success than you. Just because it happened for them doesn't mean that it's supposed to happen for you too. We each have our own destiny to fulfill. Use other people as a gauge. Let it be fuel to show what is possible. This was something I learned while scrapping my way through the NFL to become a starter. As a backup, "you're one play away," as Coach would always say, meaning that you're one play

---

3  https://www.nfl.com/news/most-talked-about-nfl-siblings-by-end-of-2018-kendricks-brother-0ap3000000931145

---

4  http://www.ncaa.org/about/resources/research/football-probability-competing-beyond-high-school

away from playing full-time. Injuries happen, but I never wanted to see someone get hurt for me to get play time. I wanted to earn it. You must earn your success. This means accepting lots of failures.

In addition to finding people to compete with in a healthy way, developing internal motivators will help provide that spark that will drive you to the finish line when competition isn't enough. Even playing in the NFL, I had to tap into something greater than myself. In my early years as a free agent, I was playing to fulfill my dreams. As I got older, it shifted to legacy. We each experience a point in life when we find something greater to play for, live for, or work for that pushes us to limits that we never knew existed.

---

> We each experience a point in life when we find something greater to play for, live for, or work for that pushes us to limits that we never knew existed.

---

## EMOTIONAL CHALLENGES

We all have triggers that make us react, think, or feel a certain way. Lyrics from a song can have us singing at the top of our lungs, stomping our feet, or clapping our hands. If you're really feeling groovy, they might cause you to bite your bottom lip. The thought of a loved one scrolling through a photo album can bring joy to our hearts or move us to tears. Some emotions are good, fulfilling, and can make us smile, feel good, or inspire action.

This pendulum swings the opposite direction too. Negative emotions will arise. This is the caution zone. When emotional triggers affect actions in a way to alter your behavior, beware. For instance, conflicts, arguments, and verbal disagreements are negative triggers that can lead to unhealthy obsessions or unruly behavior.

In competition, we had to always manage our emotions or we would end up experiencing emotional triggers. In the NFL, the consequences of uncontrollable emotions include a penalty, unsportsmanlike conduct, or a fifteen-yard penalty against the entire team. Recognizing the things that triggered my emotions and developing emotional resilience was something I had to learn. Life will teach you character-building exercises, so develop them in the difficult and uncomfortable moments when disputes arise.

As a kid who was constantly sent to the principal's office, I thought the teachers, coaches, and principal had it out for me. While I thought that they played the role of the antagonist, I was my own biggest obstacle. As John Maxwell, an expert on leadership, suggests on the Law of Consistency, "You will never change your life until you change something you do daily."

I used being the younger brother to my advantage. My older siblings showed me what to do and what not to do. Through their failures and accomplishments as well as my own, I had to figure things out. That's what we all do. I developed the character to be results driven, goal oriented, and resilient in the face of adversity from watching my older siblings. When Monsta and I finally left the nest, our emotional trigger was doing something special for Mama, especially because she kept us fed when the cabinets were bare.

There are barriers in life. Know that once you set a goal to go after something bigger, that goal will come under attack and your response to that attack will have to be emotionless. If you plant a garden, the weeds will come. There are no shortcuts to success. If there were, you'd already know how to achieve everything you want in life.

- - - - - - - - - - - - - - - - - - - - - - - - - - - - - - - - - - - - - - - - - -

**There are barriers in life. Know that once you set a goal to go after something bigger, that goal will come under attack.**

- - - - - - - - - - - - - - - - - - - - - - - - - - - - - - - - - - - - - - - - - -

Understand that your triggers will change. The things that motivated me while playing in the NFL do not trigger me the same way today. As much as I love my health, I do not like working out. Regardless, I work out every day. Not because I love to, but because the result matters. I care about vitality more than I do a thirty-minute intense workout. I do it to drive other habits in my life. In the NFL, motivating factors can come from many places. I spent more time thinking and watching film on how to be a better player. I still compete with myself. I watch highlights of the greatest competitors like Deion Sanders, Michael Jordan, and the late, great NBA superstar Kobe Bryant. When you layer their success in sports and listen to motivational words from other people's experiences, it's easy to feel motivated and replicate some of the mental work that they practiced daily. Remember, do not solely focus on performance; your mental approach and attitude toward what you desire is vitally important and, in some cases, is the driver to achieve better outcomes.

## COMPETITION PREPARES YOU FOR REJECTION

Change is one of those life lessons that just never stop coming. The choice is deciding whether to grow from it. Getting cut from the Seahawks was a crushing rejection, but rejection doesn't stop once you leave the NFL, or leave a job that you don't like, or leave a marriage that is hard. When I became a business owner, I consistently faced obstacles and moments of rejection. For example, when we needed investors and lenders to maximize business opportunities, commercial lending wasn't friendly. I had to learn from those situations, revise, and try again. I don't take rejection personally. I take it as a learning opportunity. It was a time for the company to understand its financial position. Rejection is the other side of winning.

---

> Change is one of those life lessons that just never stop coming. The choice is deciding whether to grow from it.

---

Although I didn't know it at the time, the competitive games that I played with Monsta absolutely prepared me for success in football and in business. It doesn't matter what you want in your life. You have to find a way to compete. I found it helpful to find a person or business to model after and use their experiences to my benefit.

✕------------- **PIVOT TO WIN** ---------------

# CHAPTER 3 RECAP

If you want to be the best that you can be, check your pride at the door and look for people who can push your performance so that you can be your best self. Remember to:

1) **Welcome New Levels of Competition**
   Competition not only offers the opportunity to gauge your skills but it also pushes you to elevate your game. Life will present opportunities that challenge you to do things before you are ready. The greatest teacher is experience. Welcome the new level of competition. Your breakthrough of confidence awaits your brave intentions.

2) **Embrace Competition with Yourself**
   Never stop competing against yourself. Only you know if you performed your best. Remember to block external triggers. You control your actions, behaviors, and habits.

3) **Get Out of Your Way**
   Playing or living for yourself can be limiting. Go outside yourself to compete for something greater than you. Whether pursuing the best grade in your class, top salesperson in your company, or the game-winning points, the pursuit of your desires must be stronger than the roadblocks set to stop you.

"The successful person has the
habit of doing things failures don't
like to do. The successful person
doesn't like doing them either, but
his dislike is subordinate to the
strength of his purpose."

—E.M. Gray

# CHAPTER 4

# DIFFERENT PATHS

✕

One of the greatest moments of recognition in my life happened in 2018 after I had left the NFL and returned to Southern Arkansas University (SAU) to be inducted into the Mulerider's Hall of Fame.

Let me paint a picture. My junior year of high school, I had all but lost interest in football. I was watching bigger guys like my brother have more success. I was getting more and more interested in coding, especially following the camp I went to at Xavier, and I thought, Maybe football isn't for me. But then my mom stepped in and said, "You're playing football." She wasn't uninterested in school; she was interested in keeping me out of trouble during the many hours between school's start and end each day. That season ended up being the best year of football. We made the playoffs for the first time in over a decade, and the memories with Monsta and our classmates were priceless. It landed me a scholarship at SAU, and Monsta went to the University of Iowa.

SAU is in Magnolia, Arkansas, a small town of less than 12,000 people that has two claims to fame: Having the world's largest charcoal grill and hosting the World Championship Steak Cookoff. Magnolia is small and rural, and its university is known for producing kids who want to get into agriculture, not the NFL. As a player at a Division II school, I was not expected of much in terms of reaching the NFL—but you couldn't have told me that.

After my junior year at SAU, I was developing into a solid football player, but I had one season remaining of eligibility if I wanted to get the attention from NFL scouts. I had natural speed, I could change directions fluidly, and I was a good open-field tackler, but I had to do something different if I wanted to play at the next level. The summer between my junior and senior year, that's exactly what I did.

## IF YOU WANT MORE, YOU HAVE TO BECOME MORE

If you want more from your life, you have to become more. "Success isn't something you pursue. What you pursue eludes you. Success is something you attract by the person you become."[5] The more successful you want to be, the more you must become. My mentality between junior and senior years of college was: "If I focus on myself and become a more attractive person, there's simply no telling what I might accomplish."

---

The more successful you want to be, the more you must become.

---

The first thing I did was contact my cousin's dad, C.L. Whittington. C.L. Whittington played defensive back for the Houston Oilers in the late seventies and was one of very few NFL athletes I had ever met. Tim McKyer was the first. I met McKyer right after the Carolina Panthers' inaugural season as the NFL's expansion team. Tim came to our school and had already won two Super Bowl rings, which he showed us. Naturally, we were in awe. There was something about meeting him and being around an NFL athlete that ignited a spark inside of me.

In 2003, as my junior year finished, I got a meeting with C.L., who was a scout at the time. I didn't know him well because we didn't grow up with

---

5 *Jim Rohn*

him around, but he agreed to come to Magnolia and talk to me. We met near the fieldhouse next to the football field before heading into town for a bite to eat at one of the only restaurants in Magnolia—a small diner along the main road. C.L. had already seen some of my game film, so I knew he had an idea of how I played and I was eager to hear his report. The second after the waitress greeted us, I remember jumping right into the conversation.

"What do I have to do to go pro?" I asked.

C.L. paused, clearly giving himself some space to think, and methodically chose his words. "If you want to go to the NFL, you have to dominate. You have to be the best player on the field, and everyone watching has to know that."

I sat back, took those words in, and took a few seconds to picture myself doing just that. Then I said, "What else? Tell me more."

"Move to cornerback," he said. "And play special teams. Return kicks. For you, the fastest way on the field will be special teams."

If you're not a starter in the NFL, you'd better be on special teams or you won't have a long lifespan. I knew that when I made plays on teams it would give me a fast track to taking the field for defense. It was also the quickest way to make an NFL roster. My natural position was a safety. I knew that if I moved to cornerback, I would need to spend more time perfecting man-to-man coverage. At that time, the Tampa Bay Buccaneers were coining the way defenses could play more aggressively in zone coverage, so the move from safety to cornerback was a good one for me. Cornerbacks do not play man coverage every play, but if they're good at it—Deion Sanders good, Champ Bailey good—a franchise will pay them riches.

For the moment, I just wanted to get better. As a safety, you have to be a good tackler, line up the secondary, and communicate with the linebackers. The role and visibility of cornerback, in the Tampa Two defense, uses the cornerback as part of the run defense. This responsibility meant that the cornerbacks had to be great tacklers, a skill set I developed at safety. The 2002 Buccaneers were the best to do it, winning Super Bowl XXXVII. C.L. knew I had the size and aggressive play style to master that technique and it would make me stand out.

When C.L. sized me up at that dingy diner in Magnolia, he knew that I would be able to handle cornerback. I had enough grit to make the tackles and play in the open field, I was a natural safety, I was fast, and he knew that I was smart enough to develop the coverage skills and read routes the way that I needed to be successful. In a nutshell, C.L. told me to change everything that I had been doing in my football career since I had been in little league in a single summer.

My reaction? "Okay. If this is what I need to do to go pro, let's do it!"

## FIND YOUR OWN PATH AND MARCH DOWN IT!

I didn't know how all of it would come to fruition, but it didn't matter. I left that to a power bigger than me. I just knew it was possible. I loved my time at SAU, but we didn't have top-notch training facilities. In fact, we trained in an old barn and, even though I appreciate what my coaches did for me, our school didn't have the sports medicine technology or the resources that Division I athletes have access to. It was gritty, to say the least, but it didn't matter where we trained—we put in work.

As I was in the grind at SAU, Monsta was gaining national notoriety at Iowa. It was no surprise, and we both were on different paths to the same goal. He was a starter, went to BCS bowl games, and was on the radar for many pro scouts. The athletes Monsta trained and competed against were of the caliber that everyone expected would go to the NFL. The competition level was significantly different than any Division II matchup. Monsta was in the Big 10. I called him after my talk with C.L. and said, "Ask your coach if I can train with you this summer." I may as well have demanded a spot at training; there was no way I would accept a "no."

A few days later, Monsta called me back with the news I was praying for: "Coach said it was okay." It ended up being the best decision that I ever made. Things began to align.

I knew this training meant taking my game to a new level. I was ready. It also meant I got a chance to spend time with my brother. That summer, I took classes to apply toward my major to ensure that I graduated on time. Being at school was better than going home. Graduating from college was a priority and a goal and anything I could do to fast-track it, I did. Even if it meant taking classes during the summer.

# STRIVE TO BE BETTER

Before I even got to the University of Iowa, I was in awe. Iowa City is your typical midsize city, but to me, it had big-city appeal. At nearly seven times the population of Magnolia, it was a big college town and it was Midwestern, not Southern, so the overall atmosphere was different. My brother's roommate, Jermire, was from Port Arthur, too, so it felt like a piece of home. At a Division I school, college life was different than life at SAU. I lived on campus in a dorm with a roommate. Monsta had a two-bedroom condo off campus. That summer a few of us drove to Moline, Illinois, to a Jay-Z and 50 Cent concert. I had been to concerts before, but not in an arena. I kept thinking: Wow, this is nothing like Port Arthur or Magnolia.

The University of Iowa football training facilities were the polar opposite of what we had in Magnolia. You can bet not a single one of those Hawkeyes ever trained in a barn. Instead, they spent every day in these state-of-the-art facilities that were just as good as—if not better than—some NFL training facilities. The players had physical therapists, specialists, the latest sports technology, and nutrition programs with custom pre- and post-workout sports drinks. Everything that a person could possibly need to become a better athlete.

For me, training in Iowa was a glimpse of what playing in the NFL could look like. I knew the second that I stepped foot on Hawkeye territory that I wanted it for myself, but I sure as hell wasn't going to let the glimmer and shine get in my way. I was there to work. I was there to compete and get better. I wasn't there to be someone's little brother who got in the way or couldn't hold his own on the practice field. I didn't want to be a distraction while I was there, so I stayed out of the way, kept my head down, and worked my ass off.

As cool as it was to be practicing with Division I players, I'd be damned if I was going to lose focus. I'm a true competitor at heart, so performance is always my ultimate yardstick. No matter how hard I try, no matter how worthy my intentions, if I reach my goal but do not outperform my peers, the achievement isn't as gratifying as it could have been. If I can compare, I can compete, and if I can compete, I can win.

---

As cool as it was to be practicing with Division I players, I'd be damned if I was going to lose focus. I'm a true competitor at heart, so performance is always my ultimate yardstick.

---

Iowa's football program was making noise in poll rankings for con-secutive years under Coach Kirk Ferentz's leadership and the team had a loaded roster of NFL talent. The starting safety, Bob Sanders, was one of them. He went on to be a second-round draft pick by the Indianap-olis Colts. He was a good player and won Defensive Player of the Year in his pro career. As soon as I figured out that Bob was rated the best safety in the country, the chase was on to perform at that level. As C.L. said: "Dominate!"

By the end of my time at Iowa, I saw tremendous growth in my devel-opment. I was crushing workouts, learning new techniques, and outper-forming some of my brother's teammates. For me, that was a huge win. It meant that I had done exactly what I had set out to do that summer.

One unexpected result of that training was that I began thinking like a professional athlete. I learned things that I had never been taught about the body, like different ways to warm up and activate the muscles. The coaches put huge emphasis on educating their athletes about nutrition, pre- and post-workout routines, and how to maximize their perfor-mance. I did footwork drills that took my game to the next level. Sud-denly nutrition and hydration, both of which I hadn't thought much of before, became a focus. I learned how to feed my machine—my body—with the right foods to fuel it.

I worked on my footwork and learned how to leverage defensive help when I needed it. I had to understand receiver splits, I had to understand how to read the routes they would take based on their first move off of the line of scrimmage, and I had to learn how to anticipate the receiver's break. This was the type of study I did before practice, during practice, and after practice. I knew there was always room for improvement. There's always a way to tighten your steps, minimize false steps, and get better at knowing the weaknesses of the defense and how the offense might attack you. If you want to become better, you always, always do more.

This is true for pretty much everything in life. Even if you are the best at your job, there's still something you can improve. If there wasn't, you wouldn't see people break old records. Advances in technology, medicine, or artificial intelligence would not have evolved if we had settled for complacency. No matter where you are in life, you can always get better.

## DON'T TAKE NO FOR AN ANSWER

When I returned to SAU, I felt different. I was bigger, stronger, faster, and more confident. I knew that I had done what I needed to do to position myself to excel at a dominating level and I was focused in a way that I had never been focused before. I thought long and hard about how I would convince the special teams coach to let me return kicks. I started going out with the specialists during pre-practice to work on catching punts and kickoffs. Eventually, I convinced my coaches that I was going to change my position to cornerback and start playing on special teams.

I honestly don't remember a single conversation that I had with my coaches about making these changes. I just remember knowing that no wasn't an option. I was clear to everyone that I knew what I was going to do and there was no stopping me. I would go out on the field regardless of what the depth chart said, and I took command of my desire and passion to pursue playing in the NFL.

The Iowa exercises and techniques stayed with me. Running a forty-yard dash, I'd focus on my start—"three steps in five yards, five steps in ten yards"—something the head strength coach drilled into my head. I held onto the details every day and constantly envisioned what it would feel like to be an NFL player.

The conscious decision that I made to work my ass off that summer was evident. The second step was putting it together on the field. Our first game was against Henderson State. We were on defense and the running back took off down the opposite sideline ready to outrun everyone. I chased him down from the backside and not only made the tackle but also stripped the ball. I recovered the ball and nearly returned it for a touchdown. The crowd, all 6,000 of them, went wild and we went on to blow them out. From that play on, we knew it was going to be a special season.

My teammate Nik Lewis was on pace to break just about every receiving record at the school, and we both went to camp with high expectations.[6] As a team, we made the Division II playoffs that season for the first time since 1999, but fell short losing to North Alabama. We ended that season ranked as the number twelve school in the country. I had my best season as a college athlete, campaigning my way to All-American and a trip to the Whataburger Cactus Bowl.[7] This is where all the Division II draft prospects competed in front of NFL front office, staff, and coaches in a week of practice before a game between the best athletes in Division II football. It was the best chance any of us had to showcase our skills en route to the next level.

So now maybe you understand why returning to SAU for that Hall of Fame induction sticks out in my mind as one of the greatest moments of my life. Small-school college is a part of my story. More than that, it shows what's possible when you use leverage. It happened for me. With the same mindset, you too can accomplish your goals.

## UNDERSTAND HOW YOU THINK AND USE THE CLOCK FOR LEVERAGE

I have viewed all systems like a clock since I was a kid. It started when I was channel surfing—you know, looking for something interesting to watch—and came across a TV show called "How It's Made." If you haven't seen it, the show explains how to assemble and manufacture goods and products—everything from leather luggage bags, to copper sculptures, to footballs, to balloons, to surgical instruments. This particular episode was about clocks. I was fascinated by the details of how one movement affects the entire system. From then on, I started seeing everything in life as a clock—a carefully refined system of parts that work together in order for the clock to tell time. One movement affects the other. I felt the same

---

6 *Author's note: Nik played 15 seasons in the CFL, won two Grey Cups, and finished his career with the record for most receptions in the CFL.*

7 *Author's note: The Whataburger Cactus Bowl is the Division II all-star game held in Kingsville, Texas.*

way when I got on airplanes: Fascinated. I thought about the hundreds of systems that had to work together, each doing its job, to get the plane off the ground. Everything operates as a system, and everything starts and stops.

I've been able to achieve goals that many people haven't by applying the clock method to just about everything. When you begin to understand how something works, you can work it to your advantage.

---

## When you begin to understand how something works, you can work it to your advantage.

---

Looking back on my life, it makes perfect sense that when I was in high school, I thought I wanted to grow up and create video games for a living. I loved video games because I knew that once I figured out how they worked, I could beat them. That was incredibly intriguing to me.

A football game works much like the gears of a clock. Every movement has influence on the next. These movements determine which way to go, which foot to step with, or which hand to use. Players who understand these movements the best, with the least amount of wasted motion, achieve great success. As a team, all players must work together to create overall success. The best plays and biggest highlights happen when each player is working individually to win their one-on-one battles.

In business, much like in team sports, there's a cause and effect to each move. Each department in a business works independently, but one can have a positive or negative consequence based on another department's rate of success. Great marketing can increase sales, as great pass protection can increase the quarterback's chance to complete a pass. If sales doesn't have a process for onboarding new clients or the support of IT to integrate systems, the team could fail regardless of how good the product is. If the offensive line cannot identify blitz pickups, they risk a sack on the quarterback.

When you use the clock method, you can quickly make sense of the big picture and digest which gears move the others. I didn't just go to Iowa to train muscle memory and increase my strength. I went there to train my brain. I went there to understand how football works like a clock, and once I understood that, I understood how to penetrate the system.

## BUILDING FOCUS AND CONFIDENCE

Anyone can figure out how a system works and then trace it backward, determining what needs to be done within that system to make it work. So, if each of us has the power to do that, how come so few of us do? Thinking like a clock and then getting inside of that clock and actually following the processes needed to understand it requires a level of focus and confidence that most people haven't explored. It's there if they want to find it, but they have to be willing to look. Putting yourself in situations where you are not the best, but where you can become better, will increase your focus and your confidence.

-------------------------------------------------

Putting yourself in situations where you are not the best, but where you can become better, will increase your focus and your confidence.

-------------------------------------------------

# ✗------ PIVOT TO WIN ------
# CHAPTER 4 RECAP

One of the reasons I was eventually able to play in the NFL is that I committed to becoming more. I knew that my current situation wasn't enough to get me where I wanted to be, so I got to work on becoming what I needed to be to achieve my goal. I took these lessons from the experience:

**1) Challenge Yourself**

Anyone who wants more for themselves must grow themselves first. I sought out the opportunity to train at the next level. You, too, must seek out trainings, seminars, and coaching relative to your desires. This has helped me increase my skills and chances to win. You can hit your goals by surrounding yourself with other like-minded people who inspire.

**2) Refuse to Take "No" for an Answer**

When I face a "no," it means I've asked the wrong person. Sometimes the person who says no doesn't even have authority. My stubbornness won't let me walk away without seeking the person who has the "yes" that I'm looking for. "No" could be the one thing standing between you and achieving your goal. Consider this approach the next time someone tells you no.

**3) View the End Game as a Clock**

Everything has a system. To crack the system, you have to break it apart. Start to understand how things work. If you're mindful of how one thing affects another, it can be your advantage. Think of one goal you want to achieve. What areas have the greatest impact? What are the biggest influencers of these areas? When you continue to ask questions, you will dissect the process and make the best strategic move.

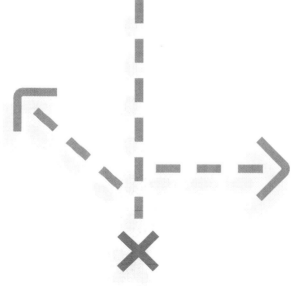

# SECTION 2
# Pivot & Play

n 1984, the Houston Rockets selected Hakeem Olajuwon as the first pick of the NBA draft. Many people know him as "The Dream." When The Dream played in the NBA, he was the best big man to use the pivot. His signature move became known as the Dream Shake. It was a fake move to get defenders to think that he would go a certain way, then Olajuwon would counter-move and free himself up for an uncontested shot. He did this all by pivoting.

Basketball players have an incredible ability to anchor themselves with one foot while feeling for an opportunity with the other. This is a great metaphor for life and what it means to move from one chapter of it to another. In life, we are always pivoting. The anchor foot is where you are currently—your career, relationships, job position, finances, personal life—you're grounded there. Like it or not, that's where you are. The incredible thing that you can do is pivot and make your next move a win. You're doing the things that need to be done to reach this phase of your journey. Just like The Dream, you can pivot to turn or rotate into a full 360 if you choose. The options are limitless.

The great thing about the pivot is that, because you're grounded in your current intent, you don't have to jump into the next opportunity without weighing your options or the pros and cons of the change. Here, it's important to speak with others who may be affected by the adjustment. Pivots can affect the most key stakeholders—your spouse, business partners, children, community, employees, customers—so having them on board is an essential ingredient in success.

In basketball, defenders are good at anticipating a move and trapping the offense. But, as Hakeem was so great at, the counter-move is to pivot again. Sometimes the first pivot doesn't work. Could you imagine having three other teammates on the court to pass the ball to? Hakeem had Clyde Drexler, Kenny Smith, and Robert Horry. When you pivot, you are constantly looking to leverage your odds, as we discussed in Section 1. How many opportunities and people did you identify in Section 1 who you could "pass" to that would help you score?

This is how I've tried to move through my life, pivoting and scanning for opportunities to use leverage. Approaching life with a pivot mentality has set me up for considerable breakthroughs.

In "Pivot and Play," I'll show you how the biggest pivot of my life—leaving the NFL—helped me identify the best way to help you overcome the adversities of change. From my failures and experiences, you will learn to navigate change better. In Section 2, you will learn that:

→ Routines can keep you grounded
→ Success will be different for you
→ Courage despite uncertainty is rewarding
→ Vulnerability is permission to be

If you want to play and you want to keep playing whatever your game is—maybe it's work, maybe it's owning a business, maybe it's taking care of your family—you have to learn how to pivot. This is how I did it.

"Winning is not a sometime thing,
it's an all-time thing. You don't
win once in a while, you don't do
the right thing once in a while,
you do them right all the time."

—Vince Lombardi

# IT'S ALL UP TO YOU

✕

he 2004 NFL draft took place on April 24 and 25 in New York City. I was at home in Port Arthur, lying on my mom's couch, unsure what to expect. I was glued to the TV in the very room where Monsta and I had made football uniforms out of socks and pillows while destroying everything in sight pretending to be Earl Campbell. I'd been waiting my entire life for this moment. Is this the day a team would call my name like I had dreamed of since I was a kid? I waited for the phone to ring.

Day one came and went, but I wasn't discouraged. I didn't anticipate being drafted in the first two rounds. Really, I just wanted to get in. I knew if I had a chance to make it to any team's camp, I would surely kick ass. On the second day of the draft, I planted myself back on the couch and waited again. As the day passed, I became more and more anxious. I remember Mom and Monsta walking in and out of the room, feeling my anxiety and trying to distract me from it, but nothing could have taken me away from that TV.

When the sixth-round picks started, I prayed to hear my name. The draft ends at seven rounds. I had one more chance. Just as I was about to roll off the couch onto my knees, the phone rang.

"Hello!" I yelled.

"This is the Seattle Seahawks. Is this Jordan? We're not drafting you, but if you make it to free agency, we have you as our top priority to sign."

Damn! I thought and hung up the phone, thrilled that I was a few moments away from reaching my dream. I started looking online at the city, researching the team's roster and which teams they played. I'd never watched the Seahawks. All I remembered about Seattle was that Hakeem's Houston Rockets beat Shawn Kemp and Gary Payton in a game 7 NBA playoff series. I had never been to Seattle, but suddenly all I could see was Seahawks blue.

To some of the guys waiting to be drafted, that call would have been a disappointment, but not for me. Although I hadn't gotten into the NFL the way the majority of the players do, I was okay with it because I never seem to follow the norm. Even though I wasn't guaranteed to be in the league, the Seahawks were giving me a chance. Not only was I a signature away from being in the NFL, but also I got there before Monsta. I knew he was a year away from his big day as well. In college, he suffered a season-ending injury, giving him another year to play before the NFL. If you want to achieve your dreams, it requires stepping into the unknown. I set my sights on Seattle and ignored all other free-agent offers. I knew this was my one chance and I was ready.

## DON'T WAIT FOR YOUR CHANCE, TAKE IT

Rewinding a few months to my return from the Cactus Bowl (the Division II all-star game) in December 2003, I knew that if I wanted to be considered for the draft, I'd have to get to a larger school's pro day. I had already worked out in front of some teams at the Cactus Bowl, but it wasn't enough to get me to the NFL. Pro days provide a stage to showcase a player's skills to NFL teams through a range of agility and position drills. I knew that if I wanted to increase my chances of playing at the next level, I had to find a way to get more visibility, which meant playing in front of as many of the thirty-two pro teams as I could.

I started looking for leverage. I took advantage of college rules allowing athletes to work out at another university's pro day. If the school is located in the same state, or if the player's hometown is within a certain radius of the school, all the player needs is permission from the coach. I had to get to a Division I school's pro day. I collected resources and began calling schools near my hometown. I spoke with the coaching staff at the University of Houston and asked if I could join their pro day. U of H pro day was my best version of the NFL combine, considering I didn't get an invite.

After working out in front of NFL scouts at the Division II All-Star game, I cast my bid, and I was exhausted. I knew at that point I had done everything within my power to get into the NFL. I had worked out in front of at least twenty teams. My campaign was complete. I had given my best chance to be seen. The rest, well, it was up to faith.

Now I had to wait for the draft. I couldn't control if my name would be called for draft day, but I got as many opportunities for myself as possible. If I hadn't asked to join that pro day, I never would have gotten in front of the Seahawks. If I hadn't gotten in front of the Seahawks, I wouldn't have gotten the call that changed my life.

I signed as a free agent with the Seahawks April 29, 2004, and was off to a three-day mini-camp the first weekend in May. I returned for graduation at SAU just two weeks later. I remember saying goodbye to friends, coaches, and professors, but I don't remember throwing my cap in the air. I loaded up my brother's 1982 Chevrolet Caprice and headed back to Texas.

This is what *Bleacher Report* writer Gary Davenport says in an article about NFL undrafted free agents:[1]

> *The life of an undrafted free agent is an uphill climb.*
>
> *After seeing the entire NFL draft come and go without their names being called, undrafted free agents sign for little or no guaranteed money. They live on the fringes of rosters. One misstep, blown assignment or bad practice can mean a pink slip.*
>
> *In fact, many undrafted free agents already received one in rookie minicamps.*

In summary: I had work to do!

---

1 https://bleacherreport.com/articles/2712980-every-nfl-teams-undrafted-free-agent-most-likely-to-make-the-roster#slide0

After all the work that I put in at Iowa and a breakout senior season at SAU, signing with the Seahawks meant I still needed to prove myself. I planned to do just that. Making it to the NFL is easier than staying in the NFL. NFL rosters have turnover every year, every week, every day. I came in the league pissed off and ready to make believers of any doubters. How did I do it, you ask? I figured out how the NFL clock works. The first thing I did during my rookie season was become a sponge. I saw guys who were doing right and guys who weren't—and watched both. Over time, I got better. Every day wasn't perfect, but if I missed an assignment in practice, you wouldn't have to worry about it happening again. Mistakes are okay, but repeat mistakes are intolerable. That'll get you sent home, fast!

---

Mistakes are okay, but repeat mistakes are intolerable.

---

## THINK LIKE A DEFENSIVE BACK

When hard things happen in life, you have to think like a defensive back. Defensive backs are known for having short-term memories. The short-term memory attitude is a way to keep looking forward despite harping on past events. I have seen secondary defenders get beat for a touchdown early in a football game and later make a game-winning play. I have been a part of those games too.

From experience, if I missed the tackle or got beat for a pass completion, it pissed me off. I knew my teammates were counting on me to do my job. But to play pissed off wasn't the answer. I had to let it go and fast. It works the same when moving through life. To think like a defensive back is to be fueled by your dissatisfaction. I have learned to feel it, accept it, and then activate it, sometimes even in the middle of a football game.

In my second season for the Hawks, we had a core group of veterans, but we were mostly a young and talented team. It was the 2005 season and we were in the middle of the franchise's longest win streak. I was still proving myself and looking to get more playing time after making big plays in clutch situations. Our team was gaining momentum, winning close games, and becoming a contender for the playoffs.

In a week-fifteen matchup, we went to Tennessee to face the late "Air McNair" and the Titans. We were a little injured in the secondary and I was set to make my second career start after a blowout win against division rival San Francisco 49ers. I went into the game confident and prepared for success, but things didn't go as planned. It was a tough day for me. I couldn't get my feet centered on the ground. Midway through the first half, I changed shoes because I struggled to keep my footing on the grass surface. Teryl Austin, our position coach, pulled me to the side in between possessions. "Hey, Babs, fix that shit or I'm going to make a change," Coach said to me. "Damn!" I knew I had to fix it because that also meant: We can send you home packing any day.

It was a tight ball game and we could not stop McNair from driving the ball. After giving up another completion, I was pulled from the game. It felt like a big letdown to my teammates. Lofa, the team's defensive captain, grabbed me by the helmet, looked me square in the eyes, uttered a few words of confidence or curse words and spit, and it was back to business. By using the "think like a defensive back" mentality—feel, accept, and activate—I was back in the game helping the team to a 28—24 win, our tenth in row.

Feel It. It's important to feel the emotion of what you are going through, but not be controlled by it. Strong emotions can swing both ways, positive or negative.

Accept It. You must go through what you feel to get to the other side of that emotion, but you cannot achieve this if you do not accept what is. Acceptance isn't easy, but it can be liberating.

Activate It. This is where significant revelations happen. Keep making courageous acts and taking small action steps despite how you feel. It may be uncomfortable, but as you gain confidence, it will get easier.

## WEIGH THE RISKS

No matter what you want to achieve, there are calculated risks in taking chances. It may not be a matter of life or death per se, but it is the life or death of your dreams, the person you desire to become, or the legacy you hope to leave. There are times in life when you know you can do something life changing, either for yourself or someone else. There are also times when things aren't in your favor and it may be time to pivot. Those are powerful moments.

----

## No matter what you want to achieve, there are calculated risks in taking chances.

----

I knew I had a chance to make it to the NFL after my senior season in college. I set my sights high and began assessing all I needed to do to ensure graduation. The spring of my last year, I needed twenty-three hours to graduate. I also needed professional training and development if I wanted to capture my NFL dreams. I was fortunate: each of the classes I needed to graduate was taught by two professors. I knew that if I could just convince two people to allow me to submit my work online, I could still train and graduate on time. Knowing I couldn't accept no for an answer, it was an easy conversation. Surprisingly, both professors were delighted to help me. I hired my first agent, Thomas Sims, and headed to Atlanta for an intense six-week training regimen before pro day.

I knew that I wanted to play in the NFL from the time I was young, but I was also smart enough to understand that for most people, the NFL never happens. The chances of getting into the league are so slim that only 1.6 percent of college football players get drafted.[2] So when I made my bid for the NFL, I didn't let go of my education. I don't want to call school a backup plan, but I knew that if I didn't make it into the NFL, I'd need something else to do. For me, getting a college degree was one way to avoid putting all of my eggs in one basket.

I also didn't wallow in the fact that I had to walk on as an undrafted free agent. I was so focused on the road ahead that I didn't even celebrate the call from the Seahawks. In fact, when my mom asked if I wanted a draft party, I said no. I felt like I hadn't achieved anything, that my work was about to begin, and that to have a party would have been putting the cart in front of the horse. But when something that you've spent your whole life

----

2  http://www.ncaa.org/about/resources/research/estimated-probability-competing-professional-athletics

hoping for and working toward happens, the temptation of reveling in the fact that it has happened is strong. We should all celebrate our wins in life.

## STAY GROUNDED

Before the Seahawks called, I had never been to Seattle, so I looked on the map to see exactly where the city was located. On my first trip to Seattle, the team flew me first class. I'm not sure if they treat all their players this way, let alone an undrafted free agent, but it was the beginning of something special, and I could feel it. It was only my third time on a plane, and I felt very kid-like as I settled into my oversized seat with a blanket and pillow. "Can I get you anything to drink before we take off?" asked the flight attendant. "No, I'm okay for now," I replied. I couldn't stop thinking about what was happening.

After takeoff I settled into seat 4E, gazing out the window. The flight attendant said, "Would you like a warm towel, sir?" I was confused, but when she handed me a warm towel with those silver tongs they have in first class, I put it to my face and inhaled the fresh scent of lemons. A little while later she came back with some warm nuts. I could get used to this! I thought. But the reality was I hadn't done anything yet, and no way could I indulge in any sense of comfort. The last thing that you want to do is get carried away in the emotion of making it to the NFL to the point that you can't focus on the task at hand. If I—or any NFL player for that matter—truly focused on the first-class benefits of being in the NFL, our heads would be too far in the clouds to even see the field.

Coming into Seattle, we flew what felt like yards away from Mount Rainier, as I gazed in awe of what is still an active stratovolcano. As that first flight to Seattle drew to a close and we began our descent into SeaTac International Airport, I was blown away by scenic views of the Pacific Northwest and Puget Sound area. I distinctly remember getting goosebumps—there was something about the skyline, snowcapped mountains, houses on the hill, and lake below. Every direction felt like an image on a postcard. That made me feel that I was exactly where I was meant to be.

The team's headquarters used to sit aside a private university in Kirkland, Washington. It was nestled between the tall fir trees and was only a twenty-minute drive from the airport with no traffic. Little did I know, in this city, there's always traffic. With each passing mile, my excitement only increased. Not long after landing, I walked into the Seahawks's facility ready to take my physical. I was stunned for a moment as I walked through the complex where I'd meet the coaching staff and trainers.

Then I grabbed my playbook and headed to the hotel. No one makes a pro sports team by standing in the middle of the locker room gawking at all of the other players' lockers. I approached training camp the same way I approached my senior season of college, with the same sheer determination that landed me here. I kept my head down, focused on improving my game, and kept a distance from the other players. I wasn't there to socialize. I was chopping wood so thin, I was making toothpicks. I wasn't there to make new friends. I was there to get on the Seahawks's roster. I was there to take someone's job.

Now, that wasn't going to be easy. When someone is signed as a draft pick, especially a top pick, the coaches are more patient with that player, and they spend a lot more time working with that player to ensure that they're successful. After all, they've likely spent millions of dollars on that player so if they don't work out, it's a big cost to the franchise. If you're an undrafted free agent, you're considered a "camp body." In most cases, you're there to give the vets a break from so many reps in practice. You're there to help them practice. Because of the few reps, it's hard for any undrafted free agent to have any real impact on the team. Bullshit! That wasn't the case for me! I was a believer and I was there to stay. The Seahawks drafted a defensive back in the first two rounds of the 2003 draft, and another second-round defensive back in 2004. Talk about competition! That's one first-round and two second-round draft picks within two years. Somehow, it didn't matter. I was determined to show why my ability would earn playtime, and it started by showing up on special teams just as C.L. said it would when we sat down at the diner when I was in college.

## KEEP YOUR FOOT ON THE GAS

For me, getting to work meant finding every single opportunity that I could to get in front of the coaches in a meaningful way. It also meant outworking everyone. In order to do this, the first thing I did was start The Breakfast Club. The Breakfast Club always met at 6 a.m., but I was normally in the building by 5:30 a.m. Before our daily team meeting at 8, I had already eaten breakfast, watched film, looked at the playbook installation, and lifted weights. The Breakfast Club started with defensive coordinator Ray Rhodes and me getting together before practice to go through practice tape. All we did was study football. Every day.

---

## For me, getting to work meant finding every single opportunity that I could to get in front of the coaches in a meaningful way. It also meant outworking everyone.

---

I knew that my competitive advantage was my knowledge and understanding of the game. I played every position in the secondary, and each requires different skills and responsibilities within the defense. That's where I won. The playbook was my playground. I learned the nuances and the tricks that opponents used. I increased my ability to recognize formations, which helps understand the splits of the receivers relative to the landmarks on the field. A wide split could indicate an inside route is coming. Learning the tendencies and intricacies of each position helped shape my game. As I moved through my career, I felt pretty comfortable owning the defense, which allowed me to eventually become a leader. I led by actions, always prepared, and demonstrated professionalism. I learned a lot not only by watching tape on my own but also by seeing veterans carry themselves with a certain type of expertise.

Sometimes you go into the game with forty or fifty different defenses in the game plan that you have to remember at any given second. If the offense motions a guy, you might have to jump into another coverage or switch assignments with another player in a split second—literally. Some players struggle with the playbook, but I knew early on that I wanted to use it to my advantage. I began anticipating offensive movements, which meant faster communication and audibles. I knew it would help me beat my competition, and having Coach Rhodes was essential to my career. Eventually other players joined The Breakfast Club, but Coach Rhodes knew if I were to earn a roster spot, I had to study the game. A lot.

Another thing I did to stand out and get better was make the vets work for the ball during practice. If I was told, "Let the receiver catch the ball," there was no way that I could. I'd make them work for it. This used to agitate my coaches, and our quarterback, Matt Hasselbeck, would give me the death stare if I ever picked off one of his passes. Coach Mike Holmgren demanded perfect practice, especially for the offense. I was a smart competitor in practice. I would never risk hitting our starters, touching the quarterback, or getting tangled up with a receiver on a down-the-field throw. Any of those actions would be a fast ticket back home. We had very few full-contact drills, and if you hit one of the team's star players, you may as well keep running to the locker room. When we competed, I worked to get in position only to make a clean play on the ball without contact.

I worked hard to get noticed because, as an undrafted free agent, you have to create an opportunity for yourself. If I got too hyped up, Coach Rhodes would come over and drop a few expletives. Coach Rhodes spent some time in the NFL as a player back in the seventies and had been coaching longer than I was alive. Ray was short but known as scrappy and tough. He was from Texas so when he talked, if you didn't know country slang, you wouldn't understand a word he said. Country slang is when every word ties together. He would come over and say, "Stay in position and keep working," but he used a lot more jibber-jabber adjectives and four-letter words to emphasize his point.

Finally, I had "the more you can do" attitude. If we needed to run drills, I was the first in line. If we needed a "look team," I was the first to volunteer. I was eager to get reps, even if it meant servicing a teammate. I approached the physical part of the game just like I did film—take initiative and outwork everyone. Every day after practice, there was always a moment to get extra drill work or conditioning, which meant I was usually first to arrive and last to leave. My rookie season, I ended up making practice squad. Practice squad rules have changed, but at that time, it was only seven players. These are usually guys the team likes but may not have a roster spot for or might need more development. Being on the practice squad, I didn't get to play on Sundays. It wasn't what I had hoped for, but this was a huge win for me. Trust me, practice squad was way better than a one-way plane ticket back to Texas. It meant I still had a chance.

I'll never forget after the final pre-season game wondering what would happen. Cut day—the deadline for teams to set their rosters—also happens to be around the same time as my birthday. The only birthday gift I wanted was to make the team. It was a waiting game. I was praying I wouldn't get a phone call from the team. It was a tense situation and the rookies were on pins and needles. I remember looking at my training camp roommate and saying, "If that phone rings, I'm not picking it up." We were sitting in the hotel room awaiting our fate. There was a knock at the door. It was a Seahawks intern. "Coach wants to see you both. Bring your playbooks," he said in a distressed tone. So, there I was, sitting in Coach Holmgren's office, uncertain of my NFL future.

"Jordan, I'm sorry, but we're going to cut you," he said. I didn't react. After a beat, he continued, "but if you clear waivers, we will bring you back on the practice squad."

I think Coach assumed I knew what that meant, but truthfully, I didn't. When I left his office, I jumped on a call with my agent to share the news. I wanted to know what it meant if other teams had interest. After being cut by the Seahawks, the other teams in the league had an opportunity to make me an offer. In this situation, if no offer is made, the team has the right to re-sign the player to the practice squad.

I cleared waivers. No other team picked me up, and a day later I was in a Seattle uniform preparing for week one. That was one hell of a birthday gift. I knew being on the practice squad meant that there would be a good chance for me to develop so that one day, I would make it to the game-day roster. Injuries happen; trades, mid-season cuts, and bad performances will happen. The NFL is a revolving door for opportunities, and I knew I would get a chance to play on Sunday.

# ONE-ON-ONE BATTLES

The great thing about competition in team sports is that every play is a combination of one-on-one battles. It's a chance to win or lose, to be perfect in the moment. It's a chance to outwork your opponent. It's the team that wins the most games, wins their individual battles more. Peaks and valleys happen. The key is: Don't peak too high, and don't get too low. Focus on the now.

This idea can be applied to everything that you do. Think of what you do every day as a chance to win or lose. You start with a plan, then enter small distractions that fight for your attention. Everything seems urgent and only you can put out the fires. It happens to us all, but remember, as in sports, the teams that outperform their opponents are holding the trophy at the end of the season. It's the same in business and in life—distractions can take us off course, but each day presents a chance to win or lose. I found out I was my greatest competitor, always seeking improvement. As it did in games, the "think like a defensive back" mentality kept me focused in the moment. Presence is the best quality to have when distractions arise and could be the one thing to help transform your daily winning habits.

## DEVELOP A ROUTINE

Football forced me to learn about and appreciate routines. Since I was a kid, we always started with a pre-stretch routine. Growing up in Texas, we'd drink pickle juice to prevent cramps. As I got older, I developed my own routine and pickle juice turned into Gatorlytes. Through both high school and college, we had the biggest challenge of balancing school and sports as student-athletes. It helped develop responsibility. In college, I always watched *Any Given Sunday* the night before a game and fantasized what it would be like to be a pro athlete. By the time game day came on Saturday morning, I was walking to the fieldhouse blaring Eminem's "Lose Yourself" from my headphones. I'm not a believer in superstition. Superstitious people believe things just happen because they happen, not because of logic, and they accept the results blindly. Yet they're only happy if the result is favorable. Otherwise it's bad luck. I don't believe in luck. I believe the people who want something in life create their own opportunity.

Routine can help increase your success rate. Someone who develops a routine expects good things to happen. A routine is simply a process of doing things that can influence the result. It doesn't mean winning is automatic, but it does allow you to feel more in control and dictate the outcome. The day I set foot in the Seahawks locker room, I started working on my routine. I didn't have it down in the beginning and some things I learned by watching the older guys, but I quickly noticed that everyone on the team had their own routine.

---

## A routine is simply a process of doing things that can influence the result.

---

If you watch a golf match, each golfer has a pre-shot routine. They envision the type of shot to hit or the number of practice swings to take before approaching the ball, or they get confirmation from their caddy. Personally, I like to wiggle my toes before my backswing. Basketball players have a pre-shot routine every time they attempt a free throw. It doesn't guarantee success, but it does allow them to envision what success could feel like by performing the same repeated formula.

I designed my routine around being the first. I had a practice routine to get taped and get to the field as fast as possible. I always used the same trainer, Donald, for everything medical related. "D-Rich," as I called him, was my go-to guy for any injury concerns and treatment. Game days were special and had their own routine all the way up to kickoff depending on if we were home or away, but being first didn't change. I knew what time to leave the hotel. I knew what time to be taped and on the field for warmups. I would always take the first bus on road games and be one of the first to arrive at the stadium at least three hours before kickoff. My weekly routine focused on recovery, injury prevention, and improving performance. It would take sometimes a full week to recover, but come Sunday, I had conditioned myself to do it again. It was vital to keep my body at peak levels, and each day of the week was part of the recovery process. Fridays were short practice days and heavy treatment to make sure by Sunday my legs felt light and fast. After practice I would get one more upper-body lift, then sit in the cold tub for fifteen minutes. The cold tub is no fun. Trust me, I've seen grown men cry trying to will themselves into 40-degree water—myself included. These daily and weekly routines became second nature and gave me freedom to focus on the game. The worst thing is feeling rushed to do something. These routine practices gave me control.

Can you remember the last time you felt rushed? Like all of us, we run out of the house with no wallet or forget where we put the car keys. The routine I developed removed all angst and tension. A routine is thinking ahead, anticipating what could happen, and planning. Routines aren't perfect and you can always modify, but they are helpful. You too should consider developing your routine. What do you do when you wake up? How do you shut down in the evenings? If you nail these two routines, it may bring the peace of mind you're looking for to feel more in control.

## SOMEONE IS ALWAYS WATCHING

The first time I was in Coach's office, I realized that someone was always watching me. Management and team personnel sit behind mirrored-glass windows overlooking the practice fields scoping every player. I approached practice like a game, so it didn't matter that I was being watched. I showed up early and I stayed late. When I wasn't on the field, I made sure I knew the play and watched my position anticipating my chance to join the defensive huddle.

Whether you're leading a team, starting a new company, trying to land a new client, or training new recruits, know that someone is always watching. It could be a boss, a colleague, a student, a child, the media, or God—someone is always watching.

As I grew into my career, I became the vet the young guys watched, which meant that they were gunning for my roster spot. That's the reality. There's a draft every year for a reason. The NFL is a performance-based business. I never fretted about losing my job and I welcomed competition. Naturally, I wanted to help other people, but when you're scrapping to make a roster, life in the NFL can be cutthroat. Real growth happened when I was asked to help teach the rookies how to transition to the NFL. When I was asked to help the next wave of superstars, Coach Rhodes and some of the other vets helped me. There was a point when I knew this was my gift to the game—humility to recognize that it's bigger than me. The game of football gave me so much, in opportunity and in life, and it was my time to give back to the game.

In life, we will have moments to share our experiences with others. When we realize that to help and teach others is the greatest gift to humankind, we capture the essence of what life is all about.

---

When we realize that to help and teach others is the greatest gift to humankind, we capture the essence of what life is all about.

---

## DON'T LOSE SIGHT OF THE CLOCK

The clock has multiple components and one move influences another. I knew a lot about football going into the NFL, obviously, but I had to learn about the business of football and how it all worked. I had to go to the fifty-thousand-foot level and take a big-picture view. I had to figure out how each entity worked specifically so that I could decide on the strategy that I wanted to use to succeed in the NFL and within the Seahawks. I had to figure out the clock.

When I joined the Seahawks, the team was on the cusp of becoming a real playoff contender in the NFC. It was nearly seven years after the late Paul Allen saved the Seahawks from relocating to Anaheim, California, by purchasing the franchise from its former owner, Ken Behring. Mike Holmgren was hired as head coach in 1999 and was responsible for turning the organization into a winning culture. The seven seasons I spent on the Hawks roster, we went on to clinch playoff berths, winning the NFC West four straight seasons and earning a Super Bowl appearance in 2005.

I knew that my piece in that clock was to be a supportive player. This meant playing on special teams and in limited pass defense packages. Knowing this, I began breaking down things about the game that mattered the most, understanding situations. Learning every position in the secondary mattered. It meant playing on special teams and earning time on defense. To explain it simply, when the offense substitutes more receivers on the field, we counter defensively to get a better match. A linebacker or lineman comes off the field and an extra defensive back comes in to play coverage. It's all about matchups. I knew that if I could create big plays in key situations, win the one-on-one battles, I would get more play time and eventually become a starter.

## MY FIRST W-9

At the end of the day, if you want to be successful, you have to be willing to create and design your path to success.

It tickles me a little bit that my first job was with the NFL. I worked for my grandfather growing up, but my first W-9 in the NFL was nothing like the $20 Monsta and I would split after cutting grass for six hours in the sweltering Texas heat—nor was my path getting there. I thought I'd get drafted and walk into a ten-year career, but it didn't happen that way.

Your path to success will look nothing like you thought it would and you will have to adjust along the way, but know that there are multiple ways to get to the same destination. I believe that it's appropriate to start with an end in mind, but it's the process, the journey, that makes it all worth it.

As John Maxwell says, "I believe God put in every person the potential to grow, expand, and achieve. The first step is believing you can."

Work, build, dream, and create the life you want to live. It worked for me; it can work for you too.

# PIVOT TO WIN
# CHAPTER 5 RECAP

Pursuing a dream is hard work! As you work toward your goal, remember the following:

### 1) More Than One Way

Just because your path to your goal looks different than those before you, it doesn't mean that you won't get to your finish line. Challenges will happen, but a defensive back mentality can help keep you moving forward. Examine where you are and be courageous enough to move through change. What do you need to accept to overcome a situation? Can a routine help you regain control in your life?

### 2) Create the Life You Want

I don't know a single person who is living the life that they want that got there by sitting on the couch. You must actively go after whatever it is that you want every single day. Win the day to gain momentum and start living the life you want.

### 3) Someone's Always Watching

Even when you think no one is paying attention, someone is always watching, which means that you always have to be on point. This isn't about being perfect. It's about being consistent and intentional. Do not let your foot off the gas. Whatever you want in life, you can accomplish. What do you do to stay on point? Have you considered an accountability person or group to keep you focused?

"Men are anxious to improve their
circumstances, but are unwilling
to improve themselves; they
therefore remain bound."

—James Allen

# DO WHAT OTHERS AREN'T

My rookie year was a memorable one. I got to play with the greatest receiver to play the game, Hall of Famer Jerry Rice—and I was on the verge of being cut any day. Practice was my game day and it all mattered. Being the first to practice was conditioning myself for when I would take the field in a game. The dimensions didn't change. The ball was the same size. That's why, for games, I prepared as I always did. Games weren't big moments for me because as a free agent I treated every day at practice like a game. I could get cut any day.

Twelve weeks into the season, I was elevated to play in my first regular season game. First, I was excited to get a pay raise! Game-day checks are a little bigger than practice-squad checks. Second, it represented the culmination of years of hard work to get to the moment I had dreamed of—running out of the tunnel to 67,000 fans. It's an adrenaline rush like no other.

I went through my regular weekly routine, but there's no question that I was excited and focused on that game day, which went by pretty quickly. We lost to Buffalo, but that's about all I remember. Three weeks later, we played the Jets, a matchup I'll never forget. It was mid-December and we were playing what was then The Meadowlands in the freezing cold. The Jets were kicking our butt. We were running down the field on a kickoff. As I was covering the kick, I saw the ball carrier running toward me. I shed a blocker and reached out to make a tackle with my right shoulder and the runner ran right through my peck and bicep. It hurt, to say the least, but I didn't care. When I got to the sidelines, I asked D-Rich, my go-to trainer, to put a soft-shell pad under my shoulder so I could finish the game. The following week, I got an MRI that showed a torn labrum in my right shoulder. I was given two choices: Continue to play or have a season-ending surgery. As an undrafted free agent, I had only one decision: Play!

I put a brace on my shoulder pads and finished the season. I didn't want to lose my job, for damn sure! I finished the season with a brace and then had shoulder surgery that had me out for the entire off-season. So there I was, finally on the roster and playing, then I get an injury that puts me so far behind on the practice field that when I returned it was like being a rookie all over again!

During the off-season of 2004, I was able to look at tape and do some strengthening exercises for my lower body, but I couldn't do anything with my arms or fully practice. In terms of my upper body, the first three months of the off-season were wholly dedicated to getting movement and mobility back. Even though I couldn't play, I was as committed to showing up for treatments and practice as I had been before the injury. I knew that to keep myself together mentally, I needed to do the best that I could physically while I was down. As the saying goes, "You can't make the club in the tub."

While the team was working the on-the-field plays at training camp, all I could do was anticipate getting back out there. NFL training camp has changed over time and league rules have reduced the number of practices with emphasis on player safety. Before the new collective bargaining agreement[3] (CBA), we would spend four to five weeks in training camp with some two-a-day practices. Missing training camp for two weeks felt like an eternity. When I was recovering from my injury, I lost timing with my footwork. I had to rebuild my stamina and get back into the speed of the game. The urgency to get back on the field was overwhelming, which is why there is a tendency to see injured players return to the game before they really should.

I was finally able to return to the field a week into training camp. I knew that I was going in playing from behind. I knew I had to re-prove myself to get my spot back. Shit, I had to prove myself every day. My first day back, I went out on the field ready to go. Mid-practice we're in one-on-one drills versus the receivers. I stepped on the field playing off coverage just to get footing and feeling since the injury, but I'm too damn competitive. The receiver ran a go-route; to break up a pass, I jumped to bat the ball away. I landed on my leg and hyperextended my knee.

When the doctors looked at the play on film, they told me that most people would have torn ligaments in their knee landing in a position like that, but my athleticism helped me escape that fate. I ended up with a bad knee sprain that put me out another few weeks. My leg was in a brace, I was on crutches, and I was worried about making the team. Sitting on the sidelines watching other players play when you're injured can challenge your inner self. Too many things happening that are out of your control. I couldn't control the timing of either injury. The first day back after being out six months, this happened. As my appetite to play kicked in, humble pie stuffed me. Life will teach you humility and I was standing in the buffet line.

# GET UNCOMFORTABLE

If you want to be a professional athlete, launch a new business, grow in your career, go to college, or do anything that you consider a great achievement, you have to get comfortable with being uncomfortable. There wasn't a single day in my NFL career when I felt comfortable. The big glass windows overlooking the practice fields, football operations and staff I'd never seen before, the media, and learning new playbooks isn't

---

3 *Author's note: CBA is the agreement between the NFL and the Players Association.*

comfortable. Not to mention the constant physical pain. After I hurt my shoulder, I was among the many other players who do whatever it takes to move beyond the immediate pain of their injuries so that they can play another game. When I say get uncomfortable, it includes physical discomfort too. It's a part of the game. What do you think happens when two people collide? Force + impact = pain.

---

**If you want to be a professional athlete, launch a new business, grow in your career, go to college, or do anything that you consider a great achievement, you have to get comfortable with being uncomfortable.**

---

Beyond the physical pain, I'm talking about never settling or falling into a state of complacency. "Complacency breeds content," said John Maxwell. Sports is humbling. Injuries happen, you lose your burst, the new rookie gets drafted in the first round, and Father Time taps you on the shoulder. Every year, any number of players can take your job. Life is humbling.

Many players felt this way at some point. I wasn't a draft pick. I knew that I didn't have any room for repeat errors, and definitely not missed time. The guys in the league are just too good and the teams are always looking to upgrade their roster. But it was my time. No way I would miss my chance. Every week, I felt prepared. Every week, I got better. Coach Rhodes made it clear to me: "Always play with urgency! Whatever you do, be urgent!" Every practice, every one-on-one drill was like a game to me. I was competitive, and I wanted to win. Compete with urgency became my routine. The game slowed down, and I made plays. The feeling of knowing I could be released kept me grounded. In addition to that, off-season acquisitions, the draft, and free agency happens every year bringing even more talent and less certainty to the field. That uncomfortable state became normal. It's what allowed me to get where I got in my career.

# CHOOSE TO WORK HARD

Two things consistently derail people from fulfilling their dreams: The "I'll do it later" attitude and distractions. "Later" is a dream killer. When I hear people say "I'm waiting for the perfect time" to do something, I ask why. Why wait? The gifts, relationships, inspirations wither away while we wait for the perfect time. Life is too short. There isn't a more perfect time than now. It's the reason you decided to pick up this book. There is something you want in your life now. Whatever you desire, the chance to do something great is what drives all of us. To put it off for later is to risk never finding your greatest gifts in life. There is no better time than now. Don't put your dreams off another day. Declare that today is the day you start the journey to something greater. You owe it to yourself.

Don't let the "I'll do it later" attitude stop you from getting where you want to go. When I find myself drifting into the "I'll do it later" warp zone, I repeat three words several times in a row: Do it now! I continue repeating until I'm doing what I said I would do. When I repeat these words, I train my brain to make the task more important. It somehow works—try it!

Working hard is a choice and it's one that you get to make every day. The NFL is a culture of hard work, but professional athletes are human too. The initial skill separation from one player to another is very small, but over time the results from the steps that each player makes from working hard can prove massive.

Take two defensive backs, both NFL quality. The difference of one step, consistently over sixteen games, earns one player a trip to the Pro Bowl and the other a pat on the back. That gap is why some players have longer careers than others. Rising up in the NFL is a game of the tortoise and the hare—and the tortoise wins every time. Not because the tortoise is faster, but because he was more consistent for a longer period of time. That's the difference.

Working hard is a choice, and it starts with a "do it now" attitude. In your role, what would happen if you told your boss, client, or business partner, "I'll do it later?" It doesn't matter what field you're in or what your goals are. You can choose to crush them, or you can choose something different. After all, it's your life.

---

Working hard is a choice, and it starts with a "do it now" attitude.

---

## ELIMINATE DISTRACTIONS

The advancement of the Internet has done so much good for the world, but it's also created so many distractions that sometimes getting any work done at all seems impossible. In fact, research shows that, on average, we are distracted every eight minutes and each distraction lasts about five minutes.[4] In a single eight-hour day, that's sixty distractions—or five hours of wasted time. Five hours! How does anyone get things done with that many distractions? For business owners, it's alarming to spend so much money on unproductive time.

Distractions will steal your time, health, and relationships, and can cause catastrophe for achieving your dreams.

These distractions are bound to happen, so you'd better have a plan to defeat them. It's the "got a minute?" knock on the door, text messages, email notifications, social media buzz, and on and on. No matter what arena you play your game in, stakes are high, especially when it comes to your time. How you spend your time determines your future.

My first few years in the NFL, I had to navigate unfamiliar waters. Nearly everyone I met had a great business idea or some get-rich-quick scheme. I met financial advisors who claimed to save and return money better than the market. I've had teammates who have gotten involved in Ponzi schemes, and agents and managers who overpromise and underdeliver. I had my share of lessons and learned to establish expectations up front.

In the NFL, distractions came in multitudes. Party hopping, social gatherings, game tickets, bad habits, travel plans, charity events, relationships, and business ideas were presented weekly, sometimes daily. Most of the time, I wanted to do nothing. Football was demanding, especially during the season. Again, this wasn't something I did exactly right the first time. Everything was trial and error, but I was able to manage things well enough to stay focused on making the team each year.

---

4 https://www.theguardian.com/lifeandstyle/2018/oct/14/the-lost-art-of-concentration-being-distracted-in-a-digital-world

By the time I got to my third season, my ego became a distraction. It was a challenge to not get caught up in the hype, especially when invitations to all kinds of events, parties, and appearances flooded my inbox. I had to check my ego and not let confidence become arrogance.

## WORK SMARTER AND HARDER

Outworking your opponent means going harder, for longer, than they're willing to go. To be that driven takes a certain mentality, driven by a desire to improve. This is relevant to anything you are passionate about. It requires an incredible amount of work whether you're in the NFL or not.

Unlike the physical attributes that define us, we choose what kind of work ethic we have. If you want to change your circumstances, you must change yourself and that often means putting in more work than you have before. Game days, for instance, were a reward. To sports fans, Sundays only showcase a product. It shows each player well conditioned and competing to win. It doesn't show you the process—the repeated hours of practice, sleep and diet discipline, going through treatment all week just to play in the game. The behind-the-scenes grind when no one is looking is where anyone can create their success.

Everything worth doing has a process. The game day is like the big reveal. If you choose to increase your health, changing your diet for a few weeks or falling for the "twenty pounds in twenty days" gimmick isn't enough. The process to reach your health goals requires a commitment to daily diet and activity until it becomes your lifestyle.

My fitness habits changed post-NFL. When I retired, I took a much-needed break to let my body heal. But make no mistake, continuous movement is critical for anyone who wants to develop a healthy lifestyle. When it comes to working out, I hate long-distance anything, including running or cycling. In 2020, with the world affected by COVID-19 and the economy in lockdown, I resorted to a stationary bike in my home. It started as a ninety day challenge but soon I was chasing 100, then 200 rides on the Peloton. (If you like to spin, high five!)

Extend your committed work ethic into all aspects of your life. If you start a new position, a few weeks of on-time performance isn't enough. It should just be who you are—always showing up, helping other people, and continuously learning. To me, this is professionalism. If you want to be great at anything, define who you are. Are you willing to sacrifice for what you want? If you are, I'll take the journey with you. There are no shortcuts.

---

> If you want to be great at anything, define who you are. Are you willing to sacrifice for what you want?

---

When you choose to have a strong work ethic, you can eventually out-work your competitor, but there's a point you come to a discovery. A revelation big enough to beat the odds. I did. I believe this one break-through helped me sustain a decade in professional sports. I realized that it was never about my opponent. It has been and will always be about me. It will always be about you too. When I made the switch from looking outward for validation to looking within, the same strong work ethic became a battle within. The legendary coach John Wooden defines success as "self-satisfaction in knowing you did your best to become the best that you are capable of becoming." Are you becoming your best?

There's working harder and then there's working smarter. Working smarter means finding ways to do what you're doing better. I watched and studied other players daily. I studied my opponents and teammates to learn the game. I studied veterans to learn how to become a pro. I saw Hall of Famers Walter Jones and Steve Hutchinson dominate the entire left side of the offensive line every season. I remember hearing about "Big Walt" when I was a rookie. He never attended training camp because the team would always place the franchise tag on him. Everyone in the locker room knew Big Walt was down in Alabama pushing his Hummer up hills. That's how he trained before the season. After missing the entire training camp and pre-season games, Big Walt walked into the locker room week one, strapped on his helmet, and went the entire season without giving up one sack. Working smarter meant becoming friends with Big Walt.

## OBSERVE EVERYTHING

When I got into the NFL as an undrafted free agent, I observed everything and everyone and started figuring how that clock worked. When I start anything for the first time, I am mindful of the learning curve. I love it when I have homeboys who think golf is an easy sport. Not as simple as you think to hit a ball that doesn't move. I didn't want to be the guy disrespecting veterans thinking I knew everything.

In unfamiliar settings, it's helpful to observe first. I watch, study, and collect information. I gather this information through words and body language, but emotion is another way to gain knowledge. If all else fails, look them in the eyes. I take it all in as any good competitor does. The next time you are in a negotiation or competition or trying to convince someone of your skills, observe these few keys to get clues.

When it comes to learning something new, I listen with the intent to be assertive, hoping to gain an edge. If I have the option to watch someone demo, that's more information to take in.

Off-season was full of competitive training drills. When our strength coach would explain drills, I was one of the first to jump in line and measure myself against time and anyone who wanted to compete. Any chance I got to compete, I wanted to win!

When you're looking for the competitive advantage, you must study your opponent. Your opponent will eventually reveal something you can use to your advantage. But it all starts with observation.

## GET THE RIGHT ATTITUDE

Success requires a certain attitude, the kind that resembles boldness and courage. It's the attitude of now. The attitude of now is intentional. It requires change. To help you make this change, I will share what has helped me. It's really simple. Repeat these three words throughout the day: Do It Now!

We tell ourselves to wait on the perfect time, but there is no better time than now. We've all done it. With an attitude of now, we no longer wait. We no longer sacrifice time for who we want to become, what we want to do, or how we choose to live our lives. Whatever it takes to trick yourself into doing what you don't want to, do it.

The attitude of now will create the change you want to make.

Imagine being a 100-meter sprinter. You approach the start line, look up, and see a series of hurdles in the way of the finish line. Your obstacles in life are like those hurdles. Run your race and jump each hurdle. One by one you will grow your resilience.

Our experiences in life help shape who we are. I can't change growing up in economic ruins as a kid, but over time I was able to jump hurdles in my own life. You can too! What are your life experiences that you can build on? The remarkable thing about being human is, we can, at any time, possess the attitude of now.

Look, you've got to suck it up! Life is tough and there's no easy way for any of us to get what we want. We must go through the process. If a shortcut existed, none of us would be the person we become through the evolution of the journey.

## HEAD DOWN, CHIN UP

Working hard and smart doesn't mean living with tunnel vision. There's a balance to it. But enjoy the moment! Instead of being present, we are often pulled in the opposite direction. We're so driven by social media and other distractions that we often miss priceless moments.

Hard work can often feel like delayed gratification. At times, it may even feel like failure. We know hard work is part of the formula to get what you want. Hard work builds the muscle and the endurance you need to push through and get small wins. Over time, you'll develop a belief that there's something better out there and those small wins will lead to extraordinary outcomes.

## AN UPHILL CLIMB

In 2005, my second season with the Seahawks, I got my first start in the NFL. We were becoming a good team. We weren't the biggest storyline going into the season, but we knew that we were growing something special. We went undefeated at home and took the franchise to its first Super Bowl. Our offense was unstoppable and loaded with Pro Bowlers every year. Our defense was a young and talented group that played together. Coach Mike Holmgren and QB Matt Hasselbeck were key reasons that we had success as a team for as long as we did. That year, Hasselbeck led the NFL in passer rating and we had the number one offense in the league.

I set my eyes on being the best that I could be. I knew the expectation was high, and personally I wanted to make the Pro Bowl. The Pro Bowl is the culmination of the NFL season when the best players from that season compete in skills drills and an exhibition game. The rules have changed over time, but to earn this accolade every player in the league votes for the top players in each position. That's the highest degree of respect from your peers. It's an individual award but can only come from shared team success. Thanks to my teammate Marcus Trufant, I had a chance to go in 2007 when the game was played in Hawaii, but never as a player. Although I didn't make the Pro Bowl during my career, I didn't lose sight that I was one of very few people living their dreams. It was a journey.

Sometimes we focus so much on winning as an outcome that we lose sight of the small achievements made along the way. I have always tried to remind myself that the small gains are evidence of progress. The course from barely making the practice squad as an undrafted free agent to play in Super Bowl XL, I thought, Damn, Jordan! You did that? I was so focused on job security that enjoying the small wins felt meaningless.

--------------------------------------------------------

## Sometimes we focus so much on winning as an outcome that we lose sight of the small achievements made along the way.

--------------------------------------------------------

I was fortunate to make it to the NFL, but my path to professional sports was no different than any other person who has achieved success. I had to overcome adversity, prevail despite being counted out, and, above all, work to be the best version of myself. As you have experienced setbacks, so have I. When I envisioned playing in the NFL as a kid, it was all game-winning plays, heroic efforts, and high fives. Although I eventually got to experience those moments, it was a series of steady gains, not a single win. I started on the practice squad before earning my spot. Yet, by the time I retired, I had played in over 140 games, ten playoff games, and a Super Bowl.

## PERSISTENCE ALWAYS GAINS

Whether in life, sports, or business, persistence is a great quality to have. Why? Because persistence is a lifelong practice of reaching for something you desire. Persistence forces you to work the plan and follow a vision. It's a lifestyle, not a one-time effort. We all have been knocked down. Regardless, when you are persistent, you always get back up.

If you have had to persist in life, it's likely you met its first cousin, perseverance. Persistence and perseverance mesh together to crush difficulties and clear obstacles. Persistence is about gains every single time you face a hurdle so that eventually all those courageous acts compound into transformation. Perseverance is to keep going, and not stop.

Both perseverance and persistence invite us to find a way. It's the "find a way" attitude that won't let you quit just because things get a little tough. A person can persist by making a choice—a chosen path of life, a plan to reach a goal, or to pursue someone or something. That same person will have to persevere to maneuver over, under, around any obstacles or challenges on the way to achieving that goal.

In life, we each will experience friction. When times get sticky, and it's hard to press forward, perseverance will help you overcome challenges. As Martin Luther King Jr. said, "The ultimate measure of a man is not where he stands in moments of comfort and convenience, but where he stands at times of challenge and controversy."

## PERSISTENCE IS PASSION

In my experience, passion is the key ingredient to cultivating persistence. You must be passionate about what you do and what you want. Lukewarm won't cut it. Persistent people are always all in. They don't know how to do anything unless they're fully immersed in something.

One of the most admirable competitors in the world, Tiger Woods, exudes passion. After battling personal issues and a series of injuries that led to multiple surgeries, everyone questioned if he'd ever golf again. Winless for more than five years, Tiger persisted to reach the winner's circle and was rewarded with another green jacket. In 2019, a win at the Master's put Tiger in the legacy book for the greatest career comeback in the history of golf.

# PERSISTENCE IS CONFRONTING RESISTANCE

Since obstacles and challenges are part of all journeys, how do you react when faced with conflict? I know I would not have achieved any level of success without enduring the pain. There is the physical aspect when muscle soreness and fatigue meet your threshold of pain. Whether or not you're an athlete, you've experienced the battle between the body and mind. We all do. The body starts to overtake the mind, telling you to stop. Don't do the extra sprint, this is good enough, I can do it later. The mind is capable of paralyzing the body.

---

Whether or not you're an athlete, you've experienced the battle between the body and mind.

---

When I encounter the mind and body battle, I force myself to do what's uncomfortable. Why? Because I am training my mind not to allow circumstance to get in the way. If we only push ourselves to the edge of comfort, we will never stretch ourselves. It takes courage to do what's uncomfortable in the moment, but making sacrifices will deepen your level of persistence. We build persistence when we experience interactions of discomfort, or roadblocks and hazards that try to derail us from reaching a desired outcome. But to act in alignment with the person you desire, the promotion you want, the business you want to start, you must challenge what's comfortable. No one has achieved anything great without stretching themselves beyond their mental limitations.

Remember, the successful person is willing to do what the unsuccessful person is not willing to do. The biggest stumbling block I detect when I run into people who experience this struggle is mental toughness. In sports, this attribute is demonstrated in how athletes emerge from difficult and competitive situations without a loss of confidence. The result: You build persistence.

I can remember many times being exhausted during off-season workouts. But when no one was watching, I would do it anyway. The mental limitations we have for ourselves are created. They are a combination of past experiences, failed attempts, and the search for a shortcut. We resist what we really want because we are challenged by discomfort. We resist the hard thing, looking for the easy route. As a result, we don't achieve what we want or become who we want. When we persist, we discover so many new things about ourselves. We uncover new breakthroughs, and above all increase our self-confidence.

## HOW TO BUILD PERSISTENCE

When I was a rookie in the NFL on the practice squad, I lifted weights every morning after the Breakfast Club meeting. The season is long, and all the strength and conditioning work invested in my body was preparation for the wear and tear of the burnout during the season. Just as I pushed my body to beef up and physically endure the demand as a player, you can practice the mental exercises and conditioning necessary to be the person you want to be. Take it from me: I had to learn through hard work to build muscle, mentally and physically.

Persistence is a muscle; it can grow. We all can build muscle. It's in the genetic make of our body. Growing muscle is to strain it for a period of time, then rest. Repeated efforts of isolating and straining any muscle, under pressure, helps expand it. The higher quality the repetitions, the longer you will be able to go. It is when the muscle is ignored that it weakens. Cultivating mental toughness is the same idea. Through courageous acts of persistence, we can build the muscle needed to become grittier.

# ✗------ PIVOT TO WIN ------
# CHAPTER 6 RECAP

Persistence and perseverance are two qualities that will help you conquer challenges. Consistent practice of courageous acts grows your ability to overcome barriers. You're a hurdler ready to jump over obstacles thrown at you as you move toward your goal. Here's the rundown:

### 1) Cultivate Persistence

We will face challenges. When we act with bold intentions and pursue our goals with courage, each obstacle will become a stepping-stone. The step to the next level is in your next challenge! This is the perfect opportunity to prevail.

### 2) Persevere in the Face of Obstacles

You're going to meet obstacles in your journey toward success. Understand that and then develop an attitude and mental state that will allow you to face those obstacles without backing down.

### 3) Do It Now

Remember, "later" is a dream killer. Success leaves clues if you are observant. Where can you learn something from observing others? Are you the best you can become? Draw the line and make the change today. Get ready to pivot. Make the decision today. Don't wait. There are no shortcuts. The only way forward is to do it now!

"A loss is not a failure until
you make it an excuse."

—Michael Jordan

# CHAPTER 7

# JUST A PB&J AWAY

M y second season in the NFL, we took the franchise to its first Super Bowl. It was a memorable time. The game was in Detroit against the Pittsburgh Steelers. We won thirteen games that year, eleven in a row. Our offense was nearly unstoppable and our defense finished seventh in points allowed. There were a lot of good plays, but my most memorable play that season came against the Dallas Cowboys.

Even though I grew up in Texas, I had never been a Cowboys fan. For some reason, anytime we played Dallas during my career, I made big plays. When I was scrapping to make the team, I returned a fumble for a touchdown in a pre-season game. In the 2006 Wild Card Playoff Game, I tackled Tony Romo short of the goal line on a botched field goal attempt. This time, in an October matchup in Seattle, it was an interception late in the fourth quarter that helped us win the game. I returned the ball and set up the game-winning field goal. There were only five seconds left in the game and that interception not only set up the game-winning field goal but also became a huge confidence builder. It gave us momentum during our win streak. From that play onward, teammates began calling me "Big Play Babs."

Going to the Super Bowl was truly a dream come true. Not just because it was a personal goal of mine, but because, as a team, we knew that if we won the Super Bowl, we would be the first team in franchise history to bring Seattle a World Championship. We were ready to go.

We landed in Detroit a week before kickoff. February in Detroit was freezing cold, but we found a way to take it all in. The entire franchise essentially moved its front office and staff from Seattle to set up our new home for the next week. We explored the city, enjoyed good dinners, and participated in media days in anticipation of the largest sporting event of the season. There were more than two hundred journalists from all over the world on media day. Those first few days had a lot of *Damn, Jordan!* moments. I had to pinch myself to stay grounded.

Have you ever noticed the thousands of flashes that happen on the opening kickoff of the Super Bowl? Yeah, me too! In the middle of the opening kickoff, as I was running down the field, I peeked into the crowd to catch that moment. The game was intense. It was a strong performance with a lot of questionable officiating, and suddenly it was over. We lost the game 21–10.

Walking off that field after losing the biggest game in franchise history was an emotionally low moment. It's the Super Bowl, for goodness' sakes! Shit, I felt empty. I played back every play in my mind fantasizing a different result. The reality was, we lost, and it was time to pack up and head home.

I expend so much energy during games that I always have a crazy appetite afterward. On road games, we would exit the locker room to a catered meal, something to eat on the bus while waiting for coaches, media, and staff to load. It was no different that time, and I expected that after the Super Bowl, we'd have a nice selection of food to choose from. Usually we were served meals that are signature to the city where we play. Like in Kansas City after the game, we had KC barbecue. In New Orleans, we'd get Cajun. So, after our Super Bowl in Detroit, I showered, changed into my suit, and headed to the buses. I was tired and defeated, but hungry. When I looked at the food table, I saw a pile of peanut butter and jelly sandwiches. "Excuse me," I said to one of the stadium staff. "Where's the food?"

With no expression on his face, the man pointed to the same table and said, "Sandwiches."

I don't know how the rest of my teammates felt about that—I don't even remember if they noticed—but getting served peanut butter and jelly sandwiches after playing in the Super Bowl, I was like, Damn. Not only did we lose the game, but we got a parting gift of a PB&J.

## HOW TO STAY HUMBLE WHILE LIVING AMONG THE STARS

Getting served peanut butter and jelly sandwiches after playing in the most-watched sporting event is an obvious lesson in humility. It's a lesson that everyone can learn. Humility meets our ego head on. Getting sandwiches after playing in the Super Bowl was one of those "check yourself" moments. Life has a funny way of delivering those lessons just when you need them. Humility's purpose is to ground us. For each of us it's different. I have had my share of setbacks and humbling experiences.

- - - - - - - - - - - - - - - - - - - - - - - - - - - - - - - - - - - - - - - - - - -

Humility's purpose is to ground us.

- - - - - - - - - - - - - - - - - - - - - - - - - - - - - - - - - - - - - - - - - - -

I passed on the sandwiches and got on the bus. We went back to the hotel, surrounded by family and a much more white-cloth dining celebration while listening to the sounds of our owner, the late Paul Allen, and his band.

## THERE'S ALWAYS THE HORIZON

I was young when we lost the Super Bowl and we were in the middle of a championship window. Roster changes happen each year and it's typical to see front-office changes when an organization appears in the Super Bowl. Directors get interviews for a GM position, position coaches become coordinators and head coaches, and change happens. That's what happened to our team. The front office went through a series of changes, and suddenly, the organization took a series of pivots that changed its course.

It wasn't a surprise Coach Holmgren was moving on, but we went through a roster turnover for three straight seasons. My last three years in Seattle ended with three different head coaches.

Yet the Super Bowl isn't the end. It may be the end of a season, but the seasons keep coming. If you want to succeed when your seasons change, you have to look to the horizon. For me, the horizon meant not getting caught in the sweep that can sometimes follow a Super Bowl. I put my head down and got back to work.

## HUMILITY TAKES PERSPECTIVE

A year passed after our Super Bowl loss, and the head referee who offici-ated the game paid us a visit at team headquarters.

Coach Holmgren sat us all down in the team meeting, as usual, but this time something was different. He addressed the team saying the ref from the Super Bowl wanted to apologize for the game's officiating. I remem-ber thinking, Your apology won't bring us the Lombardi trophy! An act of humility, but it didn't change the outcome.

Humility will find its way into our life. It offers us perspective and a moment to reflect. Humility will help you realign. Humility opens our eyes to other people's reality.

Humility definitely takes time and perspective. When I was playing, there was very little time to reflect. I felt like I was in a daze following most games. There was so much activity, so much effort, then it was over. Since I retired, I look at my football experience with a bird's-eye view. I under-stand what a phenomenal act of humility it was for an NFL ref to sit with us and apologize for making bad calls in a game with such significance.

## THINK OUTSIDE OF YOURSELF

I was raised in a small town by Mama, who taught each of her kids that small acts of kindness—regardless of where you grow up, how much money you make, or what privilege you may have—is our duty to human-ity. While I embraced every moment of my NFL career, I also understood that at the end of the day I had to look outside myself. Achievement is empty if you're not helping others achieve in the process. Life will return to us what we give it.

I believe in intentionally taking the time to consider other people. It's something I still practice today. I am most effective in connecting with others when I am self-aware. People have feelings; they're not objects.

At one point I noticed that I was bad at remembering people's names. At the end of conversations, I would ask the embarrassing "remind me of your name again" question. I meet a lot of people, but part of humility is recognizing that each of those people is important. I knew remembering names was something I should practice, so I made it a game. To work on helping me remember names, I would repeat their name in my head several times. Then I would use their name repeatedly in the conversation. If you share this struggle, give it a try!

Like many of the guys on the team, I got to know the names of the team chef and cooks, equipment staff, ball boys, and even the grounds crew. They all helped us succeed on the field and everyone mattered. To this day, those relationships are strong. Looking outward simply means treating people like people. It's an act of humanity and dignity, and it provides an overarching sense of life's purpose.

---

**Looking outward simply means treating people like people. It's an act of humanity and dignity, and it provides an overarching sense of life's purpose.**

---

I've had enjoyable experiences engaging with fans—the people who spend their hard-earned money to travel, sit in traffic, overpay for parking, wait twenty minutes to use the bathroom, and consume overpriced food and drinks, all to see their favorite team or player. I have traveled around the world to share those moments as both a player and a fan. I got to be a fan several times, watching Monsta play. It's not fun walking around New Orleans in a Falcons jersey. I can appreciate fans' tremendous amounts of commitment.

If you're struggling to look outward by always thinking of the self, consider these points:

→ Life is reciprocal—it will return what you give it.
→ Acts of kindness are demonstrations of service.
→ Ask not what can I get from someone, but how can I add value?

✗----------- **PIVOT TO WIN** -----------

# CHAPTER 7 RECAP

Once you've reached a level that others only dream about, the temptation to bask in that glory will arise. Consider how you can help others achieve their goals rather than delight in self-satisfaction. To keep yourself grounded and moving forward, do the following:

1) **Appreciate the Sandwich**
   Just when you think you've got it all figured out, life will humble you. It takes a level of maturity to notice those moments and appreciate them as reminders that we are all human. So grab that PB&J with a slice of humble pie and take a moment to reflect.

2) **Practice Humility**
   Humility is an admirable quality. When we dismiss our self-pride and narcissist ideals, we can see more clearly. This clarity will be invaluable when you need to pivot from a position in which you were comfortable—whether voluntarily or involuntarily.

3) **Think Outside of Yourself**
   A *serve first* approach is one way to put others first. It removes the feeling of entitlement. The reciprocity of helping others cannot be measured. What skills do you have that you can share with others who are struggling?

>

"For everything there is a
season, and a time for every
matter under heaven."

—Ecclesiastes 3:1 (ESV)

# CHAPTER 8

# THE FINAL COUNTDOWN

A fter our Super Bowl loss, things didn't completely feel the same. We owned the NFC West division, winning four consecutive titles, before suffering back-to-back losing seasons. In short, we had hit a slump. Change happens fast and the franchise was in the midst of a pivot. Both players and coaches headed for the revolving door. We all did. The revolving door is a door of opportunity. If you get cut by a team, you can travel to another club. The same goes for other facets of life. Leave one company and you can go to another. The revolving door swings both ways.

Coach Holmgren parted ways with the Seahawks and was replaced by Coach Jim Mora, Jr. When a head coach change happens, it's always an uncertain moment for a player. The trainers, strength staff, coaching staff, or anyone else in the building can get sent home. Coach Mora and I had a history. Not only had he drafted my brother Monsta when he was the head coach of the Atlanta Falcons in 2005, but also he was my defensive backs coach in Seattle two seasons before becoming the head coach.

Everyone experiences the revolving door. We knew Mora would eventually take over for Holmgren, but we didn't think it would last only one season. In 2010, only five years following the Super Bowl, the team hired its third head coach, Pete Carroll. Pete spent time as a head coach in the NFL before his days at the University of Southern California (USC) where his program dominated college football.

The 2009 season had been a solid performance for me. For the first time in my career, I started every game. It was perhaps my best season as a pro. I went into that off-season with no major injuries and expected to return as a starter. Just when I thought things were positioned for me to take my game to a new level, I was caught in a series of roster changes and everything changed. The team went on a rampage to set the record for number of roster moves, and I was caught in the thick of it. I had a flashback to my rookie season looking for a birthday gift of making the team.

I was entering my seventh season as a pro. I went from starter, to a salary cut, to role player. I was cut after training camp and, after a considerable restructure, I re-signed with Seattle a day later for half of my scheduled salary. I knew things were coming to an end. I knew that I was standing in line at the revolving door.

For a moment I was upset with the way things ended in Seattle, but looking back it ended with a bang. My final game in Seattle was the "Beast-quake" play in the wild card playoff game versus the Saints. The Marshawn Lynch touchdown run late in the game created an uproar so loud it recorded as an earthquake.

After walking through the revolving door, I signed with the Titans and got on a flight to Nashville. Things were different playing for the Titans, but it didn't matter. I wanted to play, and I wanted to start.

## VULNERABLE PLACES

Vulnerability is letting go. We each have the tendency to be controlled by the conflicting voices in our head so much that we sometimes act against our true intentions. When we become present in the moment, we open up and become vulnerable. We open to the fact that both positive and negative results are possible. The challenge is to accept that result even if it's not what you anticipated. This is why vulnerability feels so risky—it involves acting without concern of the outcome, a humbling experience.

---

## We each have the tendency to be controlled by the conflicting voices in our head so much that we sometimes act against our true intentions.

---

Vulnerability is hard, but it's also human to have emotions attached to our biases and programmed thinking. The way we were raised, our interactions in life, and our schooling have shaped our position and views on everything. We've all experienced a moment of vulnerability when faced with information that contradicts those beliefs. Recognizing this was a profound discovery for me.

If you are in a leadership role in your company, leading with vulnerability can be a great way for your team to see your authenticity. The same goes if you lead a community, church, or family. When athletes return from an injury, they can be timid before trusting the strength of a repaired knee or, like what happened to me, they have trouble trusting their shoulder after having surgeries in back-to-back seasons. I didn't know how much these would affect me, but I did know that one more shoulder injury would likely end my career. It took confidence and reassurance, but I felt freer to make plays when I stopped caring about the outcome or risk of reinjuring myself.

The difference between stagnation and growth is vulnerability. It's taking a step into darkness and having faith that the ground will be there to catch your foot.

Football made me feel closed because it was always a strain. It was a strain to exert so much energy and constantly defend every turf of grass. So I grew a high tolerance for pain, I became immune to stress, and playing on the edge was a thrill.

I had to dedicate myself to being vulnerable, especially in the midst of my pivot away from Seattle. Being let go was a dose of humility and I wasn't sure what the future held.

## JUMP THE HURDLE

When Carroll made the decision to cut me, I could hear the clock on my NFL career ticking. Yet despite the disappointment I felt when I left Seattle, I was still doing what I loved. The secondary in Tennessee were vets and I brought experience and depth. I was fighting for playing time, so I had to check myself. Why dwell on something you have no control over?

The only certainty in professional sports is that at some point, everyone is a former player. You don't know how or when. You don't know if it will be because of a cut, an injury, or retirement, but at some point, all current players will retire. And I wasn't ready.

I grabbed my helmet and went back to focusing on my performance. My entire experience with football had been all about overcoming adversity. Ever since I was a kid in junior high, I have pushed against difficulties to achieve my goals. This was just another hurdle to jump.

# PIVOT TO WIN
# CHAPTER 8 RECAP

All good things come to an end and we are challenged to use those experiences to grow ourselves. When we move through change, pivots in our life can leave us feeling fractured. Equip yourself for this phase by:

**1) Understanding Your Vulnerability**

When we pivot, we move from a familiar place to an uncertain one. As a result, we can feel unsettled and vulnerability can creep in. When did you last feel vulnerable? How did you handle those emotions? If the outcome wasn't your expectation, was it hard to accept? Remember, vulnerability means being receptive, open to new ideas. What would you like to do differently the next time you're in a vulnerable place?

**2) Being Emotionally Resilient**

When you're in a vulnerable place, take a moment and look at the situation logically. Emotions can cloud our thinking, but when we act in accord with our personal values, it's liberating. Master the things you can control. It's okay to feel the emotions of life, but it's another thing to let them dictate your behavior. Challenges demand for us to self-examine. What can you learn from this experience? What about the situation you can control? Whatever you can't control, it's time to let go.

**3) Grabbing Your Helmet**

Equip yourself as best you can to meet the challenges of change and pivot to win. Identify your weaknesses in your vulnerable moments and use this time to grow. Lean into your strengths and put your best performance forward.

"Change will not come if we wait
for some other person or if we wait
for some other time. We are the
ones we've been waiting for. We
are the change that we seek."

—Barack Obama

# CHAPTER 9

# DON'T LET THE DOOR HIT YOU ON THE WAY OUT

✕

For the Seahawks, we ended the 2010 season in a divisional playoff loss to the Chicago Bears. It's a somber moment when the season comes to an end. Because so many unknowns happen during the off-season, everyone clears their locker out after the final game. I boxed up a few things and donated my equipment to the local high schools. Then I packed up my stuff and moved to Nashville.

Southern food, country music, and every style of custom cowboy boots you can imagine was Tennessee for me. "Welcome to Nashville!" the sign read as I looked off the balcony of my downtown condo. Leaving Seattle wasn't a surprise given that I was no longer under contract. The Titans were a natural fit for me. They were in the middle of their pivot too.

Tennessee hired Mike Munchak as the new head coach and he assembled a new coaching staff. The new defensive coordinator, Jerry Gray, was my position coach in Seattle, and in 2011 I was strapping up my chin strap in a Titans uniform. Matt Hasselbeck and I both signed with the Titans after the 2010 season.

Moving to a new city meant making adjustments. I'd always lived on my own, so navigating a new city wasn't a huge challenge. Besides, the team provided good resources for settling in. I was optimistic about Nashville, despite knowing little about the city. I was looking forward to seeing Nashville for the first time and I couldn't wait to be introduced to the famous Nashville hot-chicken sandwich. I picked right up with the community efforts I had been doing throughout my career and partnered with new teammates to help families in need. I purchased my first pair of handmade cowboy boots that were fitted to my foot. I also attended my first Country Music Awards Show. You don't have to be a country music fan when you get an invite to an experience like that. I'm from Texas. Putting on a cowboy hat and having a couple of toe taps was fun for me.

I was still settling into Nashville, but make no mistake, I was there for one reason—to become a starter again. I looked to build relationships with the veterans and teach the young players. Every team's locker room has a different personality. Some listen to music or play games, but some don't play at all. It depends on the coach, too. Coaches encourage us to build camaraderie and the best teams have the strongest relationships. Keep that in mind as you build your own teams at home, at work, or in sports. Despite embracing my new city and team, it was a change.

## LIVE THE DREAM EVEN IF IT NO LONGER FEELS LIKE ONE

Although the move to a new city and a new team was different, I knew that I was still living the dream. I was in the middle of the most profound decade of my life. I knew that even though things were different, the opportunity for anyone to play in the NFL should be celebrated and I didn't want to take that for granted. I never felt that I was so deserving of my position or my job that I felt like I didn't have to put in the work. I was a grinder.

For some reason, moving to Nashville felt isolating. I was just coming into fatherhood and being away from my family felt like a pull. My career needed change, and I wasn't the same young naïve player that I was my rookie year.

I knew that I only had one season to prove myself with the Titans. Seven seasons into the league, I was certainly moving into the back nine on my career. I could feel my clock as a player ticking away, but I made playing one more season the new goal every year. By the end of my first season in Tennessee, I was back on the field making plays.

## KEEP YOUR OPTIONS OPEN

Understanding when to pivot requires just as much awareness as recognizing the opportunity to pivot. I don't know if this has to do with the way that I was brought up or my experiences, but I have always known that no matter where I was headed in life, I had to keep my options open.

Throughout our journey, I have shared stories of successful pivots. Each time, there was a growth opportunity and an act of faith. Pivots are opportunities to grow personally, professionally, spiritually, and emotionally.

---

**Pivots are opportunities to grow personally, professionally, spiritually, and emotionally.**

---

In 2010, I knew it was my last season with the Seahawks, so I began to ponder ways to leverage business opportunities. This is when Monsta and I ended up co-founding our first company, 2 Brothers Productions, LLC.

We launched the company when we had an opportunity to join forces with Shaquille O'Neal's All-Star Comedy Jam. Shaq had a heavy interest in live comedy shows, so he launched tours across the country. In just a few years, our production company worked with some of the biggest names in film and TV including Kevin Hart and Mike Epps.

When you decide to keep your doors open, remember to be deliberate. I knew the move to the entertainment industry was ideal for me. Since I studied communications in college, I was already cultivating relationships in that space. Even though I hadn't retired from the NFL quite yet, I knew that I needed to start that transitional conversation with myself. Whatever it was I'd be doing after football, I knew it would require learning new skills, but I wasn't ready to pivot just yet. I had to figure some things out about my interests and my future. The fascinating thing about a "figure it out" attitude is that each time an answer is revealed to you it leads to new discoveries.

As we moved into the film and TV industry, I worked to learn the parts of the entertainment industry clock. We developed new relationships with producers, managers, and other executives to influence distribution to the masses. Those connections were valuable and helped navigate a new territory: Hollywood. I also knew, speaking in football terms, that I was a rookie again. I had to watch and learn from the veterans, people who had been in the production business for years, who could help me understand the clock.

## FOCUS ON THE OPENING DOORS, NOT THE CLOSED ONES

If you spend too much time focusing on doors that are closing, it's impossible to focus on the ones that might be opening.

- - - - - - - - - - - - - - - - - - - - - - - - - - - - - - - - - - - - - - - -

**If you spend too much time focusing on doors that are closing, it's impossible to focus on the ones that might be opening.**

- - - - - - - - - - - - - - - - - - - - - - - - - - - - - - - - - - - - - - - -

As a rookie I always looked for chances to talk to the media, no matter the size of the media outlet. From small publications and personal blogs to national TV, I have interviewed with all sizes of communication channels. I began to observe how other players used interviews and quickly understood the platform. With a background in communications, I understood the position of the reporter. Some reporters appeared intimidated and would hang around hoping to land an interview with the team's star player. Others, not so much. They'd throw a camera and a mic in your face with no hesitation.

Regardless, I understood that they were there to do their job and always made myself available to the media. I used those opportunities as extra airtime to speak publicly, but more importantly, I used them to connect with viewers. I was intentional about this from the beginning. As my football career progressed, I knew more media work could only help me for the post-NFL transition.

With the end road of my NFL career in mind, I was always looking for leverage. While in Tennessee, I took advantage of an interview request. It led to a new opportunity and became part of my pivot plan. In 2011 after a win against the Cleveland Browns, I was asked to do an interview with the NFL Network. We were in the hunt as a playoff team and I was coming off a big game having received the game ball. I had set a franchise record for a ninety-seven-yard interception return for a touchdown. As I was getting set up, I opened the mic to say hi to the producers and show hosts. During the break, I asked one of the producers if I could come in studio during the off-season to contribute as an analyst. Sometimes, all you have to do is ask. A few months later, as I was in Los Angeles training, I became a regular co-host of the same show that I did the interview for. This is how I got my start in broadcasting.

## FIND FULFILLMENT FROM WITHIN

I had expected to finish my NFL career a few years after signing with the Titans, but things don't always go as planned. I was on a one-year prove-it deal with a lot of uncertainty and no guarantees. My first season I played well enough for the team to sign me back the following season. That 2012 season was my final season as a pro. It was a script that I wasn't ready to write and things didn't end well.

During the end of our last regular-season game of the 2012 season, I had no idea I was playing my final game as a pro. A leg injury forced me to the bench and I didn't get to finish the season the way I imagined. I knew it was my last game with the Titans but thought I'd end up on someone else's roster for at least one more season.

Walking off the field after the final game, I felt I had left something on the table. Not because I didn't play hard, but because I desperately wanted to still compete.

I don't even remember the day that I officially retired from the NFL. I spent the entire off-season working on broadcasting and training, hoping to get a call from a team. But, after minimal interest and only one workout, I never signed with anyone. A year after not being on a roster, I was considered retired. That's it! No retirement party, no farewell, no standing ovation—just a letter in the mail with an updated benefits guide and a handwritten message: "Thank you for your service." That's when I fell flat about football. I didn't realize my body was so exhausted from all the physical abuse. I knew it was time to pivot.

Retiring from the NFL was difficult to accept. I started playing football at the age of seven, and to think it was coming to an end was baffling. Retirement, for most people, is celebrated regardless of what they did for a living. I spent all my life building toward playing in the NFL, and then in one day, it's over.

The disappointment in how my NFL career ended and the desire to still play felt like being kicked out of the tribe. As I worked to settle into my new space and find my new identity in life, I noticed the small wins. I had already laid the groundwork for a successful pivot, but it required courageous acts in the midst of a new, unfamiliar world. I tapped back into my community. My former teammates and friends helped me gain perspective and recognize that I did have a successful career. The reality is that I came from a small town in Texas, played Division II football, was picked up as an undrafted free agent, played in a Super Bowl, and had a nine-year career in a professional sports league. All because my brother and I cast a big vision to break out of our circumstances. All because we thought it was possible.

## PIVOT TO WIN
# CHAPTER 9 RECAP

When big transitions come, understanding your behavior and recognizing where you are in your pivot can help set you up for success. Do this by:

**1) Accepting Change**
We know change is our only constant, but we can pivot to win when we create new favorable situations by using leverage. How do you react to change? Do you embrace it with an optimistic mindset or does it leave you feeling stuck? Build on your past engagements when dealing with change to help guide you.

**2) Understanding That Open Options = Innovation**
Move through your pivot with an open mind. Be creative in finding ways to position yourself for a win. Reach out to your support network, and don't be afraid to make new connections in pursuit of possibilities.

**3) Focusing on What's Ahead**
Whatever we focus on gets our attention. Life is a magnifying glass that can burn a hole in a piece of paper when it's in pure focus. You too can ignite a fire when you focus on what's in front of you. Stare into the rearview mirror too long and you'll crash. Get back in the game and pursue the future you really want.

# SECTION 3
# Pivot & Win

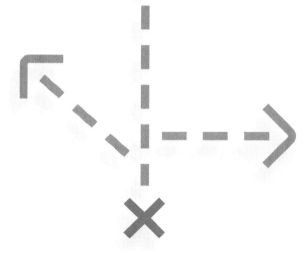

When we think about pivots, we tend to envision the really big ones such as changing jobs, having kids, or moving. These transitions cause a lot of stress, anxiety, and uncertainty, which can make us uncomfortable. Why? Because it forces us into the unknown. It forces us to take steps that we might not feel we're ready for or capable of making. It forces us to make sacrifices and practice resilience.

However, when we take a step back for a moment and really think about pivots as changes, it's easier to understand that we're pivoting all the time. Think about where you start your day (getting out of bed) and where you end it (getting into bed) and all of the micro-pivots that have to happen to get you back to where you started. When we look at pivots this way, they seem simple, manageable. But when we look at the bigger transitions, they can seem daunting in large part because bigger transitions challenge what we know, forcing us to grow. They challenge how we've identified ourselves, our worth, and our value—and they challenge how we view the world.

In "Pivot and Win," I'll teach you specifically how to get yourself through the pivotal moments. I'll show you how to:

→ Accept change without getting stuck
→ Ask the difficult questions
→ Embrace change
→ Focus outside of yourself when it's uncomfortable

Each of us has the capacity to develop resilience. Each of us will pivot many times in our lifetime. Along the way, there will be a few major pivots that will alter the trajectory of your life. I made small pivots along the way, like going from a computer science to a communications major in college to ensure on-time graduation. But, after my last season in 2013, I was in the biggest pivot of my life.

I retired from the NFL at an age when most people aren't even halfway through their first career, making a salary that very few people make in their twenties. I went from reading playbooks and studying game film to reading articles and writing TV scripts. It was bye-bye to the helmet and hello to the microphone. I went from the locker room and training room table to the dressing room and the makeup chair. (Yes, I can do my own makeup!)

The biggest pivot of my life (so far) was pivoting away from football.

In pursuit of a tenth season, I went back to Los Angeles, as I had the previous three years for off-season training—this time with a different mission. My broadcasting career was growing.

Later in this section, I will share how media was the starting point for a successful pivot using leverage. First, I will share the steps I took to move through Ground Zero, which is when you slow down and reestablish yourself in the midst of uncertainty, and how to create a plan of diffusion to overcome the mental challenge of being stuck when change happens.

As a sports broadcaster, I still watch game film on every team in the NFL, particularly in preparation for being on air. Instead of colliding, at times running twenty miles per hour into another human because he has the football, I get to inform the audience about what's happening and why it worked. The game is different when you're in the booth talking about it, speaking from experience. We call it the "bird's eye." With the bird's eye, you can see things before they happen. It easy to see what set up the success of the football play from that view. But believe me, it's very different on the field.

Are you ready to pivot?

Then let's move forward on our journey and set you up for the win!

"When you make a choice and say, 'Come hell or high water, I am going to be this,' then you should not be surprised when you are that."

—Kobe Bryant

# CHAPTER 10

# FROM MILLIONAIRE TO SOLITAIRE

✕

A s I was working to get into the NFL and throughout my career, my body got beat up. I knew football would take a physical toll on my body, but what I did not know was the aftereffect it would have.

My senior year at Southern Arkansas, I left college to train in Atlanta, Georgia. I had to meet deadlines for each of my classes while grinding out two-a-day workouts with my trainer, Eric Lougas. It was the best way to prepare myself to work out in front of NFL scouts. I put my body through intense training and when I thought I couldn't go any further, E would remind me that I was a kid from a small college who wanted to do something very few people have ever been able to do. When I thought about the goal that I had since I was eight, I pushed even harder. I was relentless!

Physical health has always been an important value to me. There are many studies that indicate how exercise promotes healthy living. A regular exercise regimen is the start to other good habits. Think about it. It's hard to eat a hamburger after a good workout. You are more likely to go for the protein shake, salad, or healthy snack. It's easier to go bed at night rather than watch the next episode of a new TV show if you know you have a 6 a.m. workout. Make exercise more consistent and improve the quality of your life. Simple, right?

For years after football ended, I could not motivate my body to train like it once did. I was active, but my body was tired. In the name of pursuing a goal, I had agreed to push my physical body to a level that was painful and, honestly, detrimental to my future health. Yet somehow, I didn't think of this physical vulnerability because in the NFL it is celebrated. Big hits, head-on collisions in tight spaces, and leg-chopping somersaults are celebrated with loud cheers, high fives, and highlight reels. When I retired, it felt good to wake up on a Monday and not be in so much pain.

I still feel the effects of these physical risks every day. I developed a tolerance for pain while playing, and some injuries I forgot even happened, but I live in pain. Yet as difficult as it is to tolerate old injuries, it was more difficult to pivot emotionally. That physical vulnerability somehow felt manageable, but mentally and emotionally, it felt like being on a treadmill, just walking in place moment after moment.

When you pivot, the change can feel like you've lost part of your identity. That's how I felt when I pivoted away from the NFL. The reality is, I did lose a part of me. Be it a new career, a move to a new city, or experiencing new leadership within a business, you must find time and space to self-reflect. This is called "Ground Zero" and it means establishing where you are. When I left the NFL, I had to redefine success. Success was no longer pass breakups, tackles, and interceptions. I had to ask myself some hard questions to do this. I invite you to explore similar ideas in your world. Here are a few questions to get you started:

What are your values?

What are your goals?

A better version of my current self is someone who . . . ?

What legacy do you want to leave?

---

When you pivot, the change can feel like you've lost part of your identity.

---

## PRIORITIZE YOUR MENTAL HEALTH

My immediate tone of emotions when I retired from the NFL was a feeling of un-accomplishment, as if I had more to do. But how could the road to achieve the pinnacle of my profession feel like a failure? The reality is that it wasn't. I had to get clarity on my own Ground Zero. The change was a disruption and it was hard to accept.

Pivots mean change, which goes against the natural behavior of being human. The brain naturally views modification as a threat. People resist change for many reasons including loss of control, unfamiliar territory, incompetence, and running from past demons. As creatures of habit, we want routine and comfort. Change is a fast way to break down walls of vulnerability. While I might not have recognized it at the time, I had some internal struggles when I left the NFL. I'm naturally a person who puts one foot in front of the other, even when the next steps aren't visible, but losing one part of yourself and then trying to find the next can be a challenge.

Unfortunately, I don't think many industries do a good job recognizing the impact transitions have on people. The demographic with the highest rate of suicide in this country is men of all races who are sixty-five years old and older.[1] This happens to be around when the majority of men retire—a major pivot. Retirement poses some profound questions. What now? How will I spend my time?

For me, undoubtedly the biggest obstacle was the psychological shift of my environment. Because of the emotions that I was experiencing, I asked more questions about mental health and quality of life. Football was physically hard on the body, and every tackle was a collision of two humans running full speed into each other. Two of my teammates had multiple hip surgeries before the age of forty. I know there is low risk in hip replacement procedures, but even the best prosthetic implant poses

---

1 https://en.wikipedia.org/wiki/Suicide_in_the_United_States

the threat of physical limitations. I dealt with what I believe all football players experience after their playing days—the emotional wake of continuous impact and collisions.

Doctors and scientists can measure the success rates of injuries. They can also predict, based on science, how soon a player can return post-injury. There are many ways medicine, treatment, and therapy can increase joint flexibility and even manipulate cells to replenish themselves. But the brain isn't as easy to monitor. It's harder to detect all of the things that can chemically alter impulses and thinking patterns through repeat episodes of trauma. In football, protecting players' safety must include all stakeholders—players, parents, youth, coaches, support groups—not just the NFL and the Players Association. Sports performance entails a combination of mental and physical health. The support of both elements of athletes—behavioral and psychological education—is paramount. Mental crisis is a severe illness and holds a negative stigma. From personal experience, interventions are necessary.

NFL players have a reputation for being alpha males, type A personalities that can just roll with whatever they're experiencing by figuring it out. But under the surface, they may silently struggle with the inability to have difficult conversations about the emotional side of masculinity. That stigma makes asking for help complicated. I struggled to find my way after retiring from the NFL and was only able to overcome my psychological war because I was willing, over time, to be vulnerable.

I did this by understanding the triggers of my pain. When my dad passed in 1991, I never processed or dealt with that childhood trauma in a healthy way. I was good at masking my feelings, even when it was tough. I thought that I was numb to pain and loss and that nothing bothered me. I imagine many other players grew up with some similar experience—a dream to become a famous athlete and buy Mama a house. Sports was our escape from unhealthy and violent environments. The NFL comprises mostly Black athletes who often escaped from negative environments. Sports were our distraction and our lifesaver. I had a teammate who grew up in Los Angeles when gang-related activity and recruiting was intense. Once, on a walk home, he was cornered by the neighborhood gang, but because one of the gang members recognized him from playing football, they let him escape home scot-free.

When I understood the vulnerability within myself, I couldn't hold back the tears. Pivots can take time and patience to see noticeable results, and mental development can help you pivot successfully. Having felt bottled up for so long, I found a release in the emotional pivot and got more clarity on myself—but it wasn't easy.

---

**Pivots can take time and patience to see noticeable results, and mental development can help you pivot successfully.**

---

## LOSS OF IDENTITY

The way we think of ourselves, how we define our values, and what we tell ourselves about who we are all come together to create our identity. Identity has a wide range of definitions. Our professional, relational, spiritual, and financial status all are entirely different. We don't always have a conscious awareness of who we are until we experience change. As the great civil rights leader Martin Luther King Jr. said: "The ultimate measure of a man is not where he stands in moments of comfort and convenience, but where he stands at times of challenge and controversy." In our moments of discomfort, particularly when we're in a pivot, deciding to change helps us focus our lens inward guided by our personal values.

When going through a transition, really spend some time better understanding those identities because the loss of any one can create an emotional domino effect. Research has shown the lack of self-clarity that comes in grief as a result of a loss of identity relates to higher rates of depression and post-traumatic stress.[2] It's essential to remain aware and respectful of how hard transitions can be, but you, too, can have a successful pivot after establishing your new Ground Zero.

---

2 *https://www.nimh.nih.gov/health/publications/post-traumatic-stress-disorder-ptsd/index.shtml*

# TRANSITIONS CANNOT BE AVOIDED

Anyone who moves toward a goal with voracity knows somewhere in the back of their mind that painful transitions are unavoidable. I knew when Monsta and I were knocking each other down in my mom's house that once I got into the NFL, I'd eventually leave the NFL. In some way I think athletes come to terms with this inevitability quicker than other people because we know that physiologically, we simply won't be able to do what we're doing until the end of our lives. That being said, anyone who is working toward a goal diligently will have to transition in some way once that goal is met.

If you have difficulty getting your head around transitions, break them down. Instead of looking at the big transition down the road—the one that you know will come but doesn't tell you what's on the other side—pay attention to the dozens of small transitions you make every single day. Getting out of bed in the morning, putting your feet on a cold floor, and having to move into the bathroom is a transition from rest and relaxation to momentum. The commute from home to work, work to lunch, and back to the office is a series of micro-pivots. Even if you work from home, it requires a process to jump into "work mode." Leaving work and then walking into family life is another micro-pivot from being one person (employee) to being another (parent).

When I experience these minute changes throughout the day, I take a little quiet time before entering a new setting in what I call the "buffer zone." The buffer zone helps me digest thoughts so that I can transition into new environments and conversations as a better person. You can do this in your car and in between phone calls by setting up two to three minutes of space. We transition all day from phone call to meeting to email and never pause to create head room. Time is important and that buffer zone can help you transition better throughout the day.

I understand what it means to go through days with the mental angst and pressure of performing at work, only to then have to flip the switch to become a joyful parent or loving spouse. It has its challenges, but remember other people are counting on you and dragging work stress into the home can become toxic. As you go through the day today, notice the micro-pivots you experience and be open to the buffer zone. It happens daily, and I have used this simple technique to help myself transition. Try it. It works for me—see if it helps you.

## PLANNED VS. UNPLANNED PIVOTS

While we know that change will happen, the process of moving through that transition or pivot may differ depending on whether the transition was planned or unplanned. Planned transitions often give us a little more time to think through how we want to move through them and exert some level of control. Unplanned transitions—unexpectedly losing a job, experiencing the death of a close family member—put us in a reactive state.

When you're experiencing an unplanned transition, try to remember that even planned transitions have an element of surprise. No matter how well we plan, we can't predict the future. Do the best you can with the information you have, go easy on yourself as you move through the transition, and keep moving forward with intention. Finally, stay open to discovery. You never know what new opportunities your transition might bring.

## IT'S OKAY TO FEEL STUCK

Even though you must keep moving through a transition to reinvent yourself, it's completely normal to feel stuck. They key is to not stay stuck. I don't think we give ourselves enough permission to be where we are sometimes. Give yourself permission to just be. During my first season of retirement, there were times of uncertainty and moments of feeling stuck. The things I once knew were now different. I was grappling with bigger questions like, "Who am I? What should I be doing? How can I contribute?"

---

Even though you must keep moving through a transition to reinvent yourself, it's completely normal to feel stuck. They key is to not stay stuck.

---

There's a difference in feeling stuck and staying stuck. Staying stuck is an inability to see the forest for the trees. It means you're focusing too much on negative thoughts and getting caught replaying the cycle of pain, hurt, or letdown. The fact is: Life promises struggle. We all face challenges. At the core of those thoughts and feelings lies the enemy to defeat: Fear. You don't have to feel inadequate; you have already accomplished and overcome many other challenges in your life. Keep moving through the pivot.

There are multiple ways to move from a stagnant position to action. Being stuck is a combination of mental and physical limitations we place on ourselves. These are false beliefs. Talking it out with a professional therapist, friend, respected colleague, or mentor is one method to generate movement. When we hear ourselves talk through those barriers, it can be self-revealing.

Another way to go from stagnation to action—a technique I have seen when people want to plan a career path—is called reverse engineering. The idea of starting with an end in mind by casting a big vision and working backward can give you clarity on which first step to take. These three questions can help you get started.

→ Think about what you really want in life "someday" and write it down.
→ Ask yourself what someone in this role does every day. What relationships and conversations are they having daily that I am not?
→ What can I do now to become that person I envision for myself?

Gary Keller and Jay Papasan reveal a great reverse engineering method in their book *The One Thing*, which I have used to get better clarity of the "lead domino." There are no limits. Sometimes our vision of ourselves can seem so big we do nothing, so go small. There is no easy way. An unstuck person gets there because they have vision. Proverbs warns us: "Where there is no vision, the people perish."[3] If all you see is what you can see with your eyes, you do not see all there is to be seen.

To do this, we must each put one foot in front of the other and set a vision, even if it seems uncertain how it might be fulfilled. This attitude of belief is how I "worked" myself into the NFL.

---

3 *Prov. 29:18*

As I was navigating the biggest pivot of my life, from pro athlete to entrepreneur and business executive, I got up early in the morning when I didn't feel like it just to get a head start on the day. I didn't always know exactly what to work on, so I would generate energy by working out and became intentional about self-care and learning. Podcasts, seminars, and audiobooks filled my earbuds as I performed thirty- to forty-minute workouts. After training for so long, working out is something I don't like to do anymore, which is exactly why I do it.

To continue moving through the feeling of being stuck, I called close friends, teammates, and other people I looked up to even when the timing wasn't perfect. I attended events with the intent to engage in more fulfilling conversations. Trust me, those were better than the negative self-talk that was happening in my head. "Life is about not knowing and doing something anyway," someone shared with me. Eventually, by forcing myself into those actions and environments, I overcame being stuck. I began to feel an increase of vitality and life.

If you're feeling stuck, live by that quote and do something anyway. The answers will reveal themselves. Walk through your days even when the thought of progress seems impossible. You must keep moving.

## GET REAL WITH YOURSELF

When I first began to transition out of the NFL, I was still in a bit of a haze. My body desperately needed rest, and mentally I was trying to figure out how to move through the change. I had to slow down. The unknown is another reason to resist change, and I was looking through a lens of uncertainty. I felt like I had fallen down the rabbit hole in *Alice in Wonderland* and when I looked around, every face seemed unfamiliar.

It was hard to talk to people about these feelings. Why? Because I resisted asking for help. Instead, I wanted to do it myself. I thought I could figure it out alone. But what causes us to think that we are alone in our situations? I discovered that doing this alone creates a toxic explosion.

In other words, express yourself. Let it out and let it go. It does more harm to yourself to hold onto past resentments and the things you cannot control. Because I was so unused to asking for help, it was hard to start talking to people about these feelings and questions. But I knew that in order to move through them, I had to let my guard down, ask for help, and be more vulnerable. I had to emerge from a shield of toughness and masculinity to welcome openness. When I did this, I realized that my heart had hardened a little bit during my NFL career. I guess that's because in that industry, a person is expected to mask anything that isn't toughness. Trying to dial into that softer side took a lot of work because it's an internal battle.

---

## I had to emerge from a shield of toughness and masculinity to welcome openness.

---

While I was going through this process, I realized that I had to stop giving a shit. Not about my family or my goals, but about what others thought of me. So what if I needed help? The only way to be vulnerable is to meet vulnerability head on. Once I let my guard down and allowed myself to become vulnerable, wisdom started coming at me from unexpected places.

It was like a huge weight dropped off me. I was able to let go of so many thoughts and feelings and worries that really didn't matter. This transformation also forced me to look at my habits and decide which were serving me and which weren't. As I started creating a vision for what I wanted my life to look like, I had to let go of habits that wouldn't move me in that direction and adopt others that would.

---

## As I started creating a vision for what I wanted my life to look like, I had to let go of habits that wouldn't move me in that direction and adopt others that would.

---

I picked up the habit of creating daily think time to calm my thoughts and learned to be more patient, especially with myself. I started time blocking better and became more intentional about life and the lifestyle that I desired for myself and family. Much-needed escapes to "paradise," which for me is the golf course, also helps. Something about the sport of golf helps me get centered. I have teammates and friends who love to fish and find their paradise on the water. What's your paradise? A trip to your paradise may be what you need right now. Care for yourself better and take time to think. You deserve it.

## TAKE A MOMENT TO BREATHE

The biggest pivot of my life—transitioning from the NFL into another career—required a lot of breathing on my part. I knew that I would eventually leave the NFL, but that knowledge didn't lessen the blow once it happened. I thought to myself, I knew this was coming, but I thought it would look a lot different than this. I still don't know what I expected "this" to be, but I know that when I was navigating the change, the direction I was headed in didn't feel right. It didn't feel right because of the emotional wake of playing nine seasons of professional football. Around this time, I was living in Los Angeles part-time and working at the network. I rented a small condo in Hollywood, near Runyon Canyon. Early mornings consisted of walking to the top of the trails, which was another way that I found space to breathe.

Transitioning out of the NFL felt like a long breakup with football. There's something special about running out of the tunnels and performing for fans while also putting yourself in a ring of top-tier competition. It's living on the edge because you have to make the right decisions instinctively within a tenth of a second. Football takes a tremendous amount of stamina. NFL games are sixty minutes and can range from sixty-five to seventy-five plays on offense and defense and ten to fifteen-plays on special teams. We learn to control our breathing so that we don't exhaust ourselves too quickly. Then there's the fourth quarter, when the game is on the line.

In football and every other sport, the best athletes thrive in moments that feel tense to others. This is because they have control of their breathing. It's not something you can only do in the game; it takes practice. Lots of practice. When moments like taking the game-winning shot or kicking the game-winning field goal seem automatic, these athletes win because they're trained to take longer and slower breaths.

I spent a lot of time breathing while trying to get comfortable with whatever direction my life was moving in. It's what I've always done, but off the field, for me, this means spending moments of the day in silence. I usually do this in my morning routine before the craziness of the day starts. Sometimes I do this by reading a book; other times I just invite stillness. These moments of reflection are a much-needed check-in with myself.

There's a huge exploration process that transitions encourage. For me, being able to sit in that exploratory space took a lot of practice, vulnerability, and breath. I still sit in my car for a few minutes after work before I drive home to consciously transition from the work part of my day to the family part of my day.

## FIND A GOOD GROUP OF PEOPLE

One of the most effective ways to create a successful pivot is to find people who are supportive of that transition. We are creatures of habit, so it's easy to get comfortable in your company even though you really desire to start your own business. It's comfortable to guard your feelings because you've been hurt in the past, but you really desire a loving relationship. It's comfortable to binge-watch TV even though you want more vigor in your life. We've all been there. When I was in the warp of change, it had an effect on other people, sometimes without me even realizing it.

- - - - - - - - - - - - - - - - - - - - - - - - - - - - - - - - - - - - - - - - - -

One of the most effective ways to create a successful pivot is to find resources and people that are supportive of that transition.

- - - - - - - - - - - - - - - - - - - - - - - - - - - - - - - - - - - - - - - - - -

When I set out to find my new community after football, I was intentional about the people who I wanted to spend time with. I attended social and charity events to connect with other community and business leaders. It isn't easy, but it will happen if you focus on looking for people who share your values. Sometimes finding what you value in a person means finding what you don't value.

Find people who see you for the person you desire to be. For me, as it is for you, there is a community of people who appreciate you and want to see you succeed. As I often remind myself, spend more time with them. Share your vision, dreams, and goals with them. Your community of supporters will help you succeed.

Jim Rohn was right when he said, "You are an average of the five people you spend the most time with."

## FIND RESOURCES THAT WORK FOR YOU

My pivot from the NFL landed me in the broadcast arena, a natural fit after studying communications as an undergrad. I was already a business owner but there was still so much to learn. I was interested in soaking up as much as I could about broadcasting and operating a business. I recognized that I had knowledge gaps in both, so I became intentional about subject-specific learning to help generate ideas. You should know that if you ever go on a road trip with me, I will always play an audiobook, seminar, or podcast. Driving is a perfect time to learn.

At times, it felt like I was reading the instruction manual and flying the airplane at the same time. Make one adjustment, a fuse blows. Get the fuse fixed, the water begins to leak. That's how I felt running a business early on. Books and podcasts helped but only so much. I decided to invest in personal training and development so that I could be among other like-minded, high-performance, results-driven maniacs like me. Weirdos, like yourself. We're alike.

Then, as if all the videos and seminars weren't enough, I enrolled in grad school to pursue an MBA. If you can't tell by now, I am notoriously driven by the things I am passionate about. Each step, failures included, is part of the process. Fail your way to success! I love an environment that forces me to elevate. I crave to be around elite talent because that's what I expect from myself.

Never miss an opportunity to learn something new. When people make book recommendations, I check to see if it's a book to add to my library. When someone recommends a podcast or inspirational video, I listen. Why? Because you never know the one idea that will change the course of your life forever.

I'll never forget the day I joined a webinar session around the topic of business with a group of other former NFL players. I was a few miles east of Seattle, parked at a drive-through burger joint. On that call, I got the idea that has helped shape the rest of my life. Someone recommended *The Entrepreneur Roller Coaster* by Darren Hardy. I immediately downloaded and read the book, and it became an invaluable resource to help me pivot. It started a swell of positive energy and I could feel momentum growing to become a better me.

I eventually met Darren after an intense three-day high-performance training seminar in La Jolla, California. Darren introduced me to his mentor, the late Jim Rohn, a "farm boy from Idaho," and began sharing his teachings with me. Jim told me, through his audio recordings of course, "Success is something you attract by the person you become; what's easy to do is easy not to do." For weeks at a time, I listened to his teachings to initiate and develop other behavior changes that would help me reach new levels and transform. Creating good habits means challenging the status quo through repetitive, deliberate, and intentional actions.

## RESPECT THOSE WHO HAVE COME BEFORE YOU

Here's a hell of a transition: Getting a phone call that the father of your children has died and being told that you will not only have to raise five kids on your own but also have to make enough money to support those kids. Now, who wants to go on from that? I could tell from my mom's tears and stress during that time that she wasn't excited about the unplanned transition—but she faced it. She found a way to earn a good enough living to get all of us through college. Despite the odds that were stacked against her, she found a way through. When I think about my mama, the thing that I most want to do is continue moving the needle forward for my family.

If you're struggling to get through a transition, think about the people who have gone before you. Think of those who have found it within themselves to push through the adversity and uncertainty that they faced during a dramatic transition. You, too, can overcome adversity and pivot to success.

- - - - - - - - - - - - - - - - - - - - - - - - - - - - - - - - - - - - - - - -

If you're struggling to get through a transition, think about the people who have gone before you.

- - - - - - - - - - - - - - - - - - - - - - - - - - - - - - - - - - - - - - - -

## LET THE PROCESS PLAY OUT

Pivoting is a process. As much as we'd like to have it happen overnight, I promise you it doesn't. Recognize that this process is going to take time and it's going to meet some successes and some failures. Those three things—time, success, and failure—are all a part of the process. They can't be skipped; they can't be sped up. They have to be recognized, felt, and then moved through.

## BREAK THE CONFLICT INTO MEASURABLE RESULTS

After establishing my new Ground Zero, I found a way to view change in a practical way to prepare for the pivot.

1) I **discovered** new purpose
2) I **pruned** for growth
3) I **changed** through the pivot

### DISCOVER

I believe we each are here for a designed purpose, to make a dent in the universe and do good for humanity. Some figure it out sooner than others, but the point is, it's never too late to discover your purpose.

### PRUNE

Pruning is a process that we usually relate to roses, hydrangeas, or apple trees, but what does it mean to prune your life? As it relates to gardening, pruning is when you selectively remove branches from a tree to improve healthy growth. Pruning clears out dead, diseased, and damaged limbs to give the tree a polished look, which allows it to grow to its full potential. Now, think about pruning in your life. Where can you cut? Where can you create room for more growth?

## CHANGE

Once you've established Ground Zero and reconnected with (or found) your purpose, make a list of the changes that you need to make to move into the next iteration of your best self. This was a largely habit-based experience for me. I knew certain behaviors needed to change in my life.

✗----------- **PIVOT TO WIN** -----------

# CHAPTER 10 RECAP

Retiring from the NFL and moving into a new career was one of my life's biggest pivots, but it's only one of many that I'll make in this lifetime. No matter who you are, what you do for a living, how much money you make, how many kids you have, or where you live, life will alter your path and you will pivot. Sometimes it will be planned, other times unplanned. Either way, the key to the pivot is you.

If you're going through a transition, focus on these four things:

### 1) Not Staying Stuck
You can feel stuck, you can complain about being stuck, but once the emotion passes, get to work! Focus on finding resources that are uplifting and give you hope. Be kind to yourself and focus on the image of your better self. When days don't feel great, go to paradise. Train your mind to think about greatness. Beating yourself up won't get you anywhere.

### 2) Being Vulnerable
Are there areas in your life that feel guarded? To be vulnerable means to challenge our insecurities. When we explore these thoughts of self-doubt, it's crucial to understand how they make us think. Sometimes the feeling of embarrassment can be the reason to drive change. Remember, we are moving toward the best version of you. Take an honest inventory of areas to prune, and ask others for help.

### 3) Examining Your Behaviors
Change is constant. We must be intentional about growing ourselves, even during a pivot. Consider developing new

skills and new relationships that support your discoveries in Ground Zero. The first step to change is looking at your behaviors. What activities do you do in a day, a week, or a month? Once you create a list of those behaviors, it will be easier to see what stays and what goes. Which of these activities is serving you? Which will you give up in pursuit of something more? Find your balance.

### 4) Trust the Process

I have used failure as a stepping-stone to reach new levels. Small setbacks happen, but don't beat yourself up over it. Learn from them. Each obstacle builds resilience and belief. You are not the same person today as you were yesterday. You will not be the same person one year from today. Let's continue the journey together.

"A man who views the world the same at 50 as he did at 20 has wasted 30 years of his life."

—Muhammad Ali

# NEAUX YOUR ROLE

✕

In 2014 when I transitioned out of the NFL, life drastically changed. With those changes came an overwhelming shift in my perspective on accomplishing goals, continuing my personal development, and mastering new skills. It also became clear that life is not about the grind. This realization didn't happen overnight, but by committing to improving myself and learning how to shift what I was thinking about and how I saw myself, I was able to keep progressing.

In 2011, when I was playing in Tennessee, we were on the road against the Cleveland Browns. Late in the game, I returned an interception for ninety-seven yards for a touchdown. At the time, it was the fourth-longest pick-six in franchise history. The next morning, I was interviewed on the NFL Network about the big win. During the commercial break, I began speaking with network producers about coming to the studio during the upcoming off-season. I saw an opportunity—I would already be training in Los Angeles, so why not start getting more camera time? It was also a way to connect with people who were in the broadcast industry, which I thought might help me pivot once my time in the NFL was finished.

Sports broadcasting was the first opportunity after I retired from the NFL to move forward into the known. It was the first time since football that I had created an opportunity for myself, and it happened because I followed a simple truth: "Ask, and you shall receive."

## ALL YOU HAVE TO DO IS ASK

Kids are some of the most curious creatures on the planet. Parents know that this can be either annoying or cute. It depends on the day, the parent, and the child. As the youngest sibling in my family, I was pushed by my brothers to be vocal. It was their way of forcing me to get comfortable with figuring things out by myself.

Somehow when we get older, we stop asking for things, yet many doors open when you continue to ask.

In 2011, I was into year eight of my career, my contract with the Seahawks had ended, I wasn't signed to any team, and the NFL and NFL Players Association were unable to reach a new collective bargaining agreement—meaning lockout. Being that I was a free agent, it wasn't the best time to be on the market. It meant that signing with a team would be unlikely to happen before the start of training camp. I, like many other players, spent off-seasons in Los Angelese training. But every player looking to make a roster that season was unable to have a team off-season program. The lockout prohibited access to team facilities. While I was in Los Angeles during the lockout, I took advantage of downtime. The NFL Network is the right way for players who are interested in the media to break into the broadcast industry. That's when I started working on the morning show *NFL AM*. The show was all things NFL, from breaking news, to highlights, to interviews with players.

From there, I started working with a speech coach and attending events where I might meet other people of influence. The idea was to build relationships in a new city. That period of time was a Ground Zero moment. When I began contributing as an analyst on the morning show, we had production meetings at 1 a.m. I was in the makeup chair around 2 a.m. and on set from 3 a.m. to 7 a.m. every weekday morning talking football. At Ground Zero, I was earning my stripes as a broadcaster on the graveyard crew. It was hard as hell going to bed in the middle of the day in Los

Angeles. While the time of day for broadcasting wasn't exactly ideal, I knew that developing my on-air personality was most important. Hey, I thought, you started on the practice squad. I got my first gig on the NFL Network and was willing to start at Ground Zero. That's how *NFL AM* became a stepping-stone to a new career in broadcast.

## PLAY TO YOUR STRENGTHS

I never had a nervous moment during my broadcast career. I had studied broadcast in school, I had made a point to talk to and work with the media while I was a player, and I was confident that I had the skills needed to get the job done.

When it's time to make a transition, especially if it's an unexpected transition, put your energy behind things that will naturally bring you the most success. Choose those things, and then figure out how to get better at them. Even though I had confidence in communicating for a large audience, being an analyst is its own skill set, and I knew, I had to add it to my repertoire.

---

> When it's time to make a transition, especially if it's an unexpected transition, put your energy behind things that will naturally bring you the most success.

---

Analysts are paid to deliver the truth. They are also paid for their personality and the unique way that they deliver views and opinions on the game to an audience. Interacting with the audience is really about helping increase their knowledge without using too much inside lingo. You want everyone to feel included, even if they don't know that much about football, so that they have some degree of understanding.

I had studied broadcast journalism in college, but being an analyst was still a new career path for me. I still had to learn, and I did that every day. Just like when I was a player, after each show I would look at my tape, make a list of takeaways, and then develop a plan for improving my performance. As Jim Rohn would remind me, "Repetition is the mother of skill." If you want to be good at anything, it requires practice. As a speaker, reading out loud was my fundamental skill. Improving meant removing a specific tone or word from my way of speaking or changing my hand movements (too many hand movements can be distracting to the viewer). Every day I made small adjustments to my presentation and practiced my breathing exercises because I wanted to see that repetitive effort work—and it did!

Another thing I had to learn was that, as an analyst, it's okay to disagree. To a player, protecting the team is habitual. It's the number one rule especially for those of us who have played under Pete Carroll. As an analyst, I was required to look at the game through a different lens. Viewers and fans expect analysts to form opinions and provide evidence. I had to learn to be honest in my analysis without dogging players. I understood how hard it was to make every play, but I also wanted to explain why one team would perform better than another. In other words, I was finding my style to entertain and educate the viewer.

Not long after I started analyzing for the Hawks, I felt like I had returned to the game, but in a different way. Every week, I had to understand what was happening with the players, the game, and their opponents so that on Sunday, I could deliver for the game. Just like I did when I was a player, I watched the film, I took notes, I talked to the coaches, I talked to the players, and I watched the dynamics among team members. Scouting and game prep by analyzing teams are all about gearing up for execution. Take what you know, figure out how to do it better, and then focus on moving the ball down the field.

## FOCUS ON YOUR GRIT

While I was transitioning into my new roles, there were moments when I had to focus on the grit that I had developed as a football player. I have been developing grit my entire life. I grew up in uncertain circumstances where food was often scarce, and I overcame the biases and beliefs of others. By the time I pivoted away from football, grit was innate in me. Grit is something each one of us can develop by continually overcoming inadequate conditions. Whether mentally overcoming the need to speak up about injustice or gaining the courage to overcome life-altering pivots, having grit is a skill that requires extreme perseverance, and it's one that helped me get through mental and physical challenges associated with significant pivots.

---

**Grit is something each one of us can develop by continually overcoming inadequate conditions.**

---

Anytime I felt a struggle coming on during my broadcast career, I would focus on the tools and mindset that I used to overcome unknowns during my football career. This includes my road as an undrafted free agent, injuries that jeopardized my career, and many other barriers I surpassed. My thought about broadcasting was: Why would this be any different just because it's a new territory? In revisiting these moments, I was able to focus on the grit that was required to move through these hardships.

## CHECK IN WITH YOURSELF

When you're in your pivot, and the next steps seem unsteady or unsure, it's easy to go with the flow of whatever's coming your way. Beware, there's a danger in doing that. The risk is conformity. When you conform, you subtly drift off-track rather than being intentional about where you want to go. My thought is: If you've gotten this far, don't look back now!

Just because I felt confident working in media didn't mean doing it felt fulfilling. I had moments when I asked myself, "Jordan, are you on the right path?" It was difficult after playing in the NFL to start over again. There were also times when I felt like I was ready for and needed to move into a more prominent role with more responsibilities.

Pivots are like that for everyone, though. It's just the nature of starting something new.

In addition to figuring out my next career move, I started seeking deeper meaning in my life. Retiring in your thirties leaves a lot of room for living, and I had a strong personal desire to be something more than an NFL player. Football is part of my identity, but knowing my kids will never remember me for my days as an athlete is a reason to strive for greater things in life. When I became a parent, I pivoted in my thinking. I became intentional about more purposeful things. Although I didn't know if broadcast was going to be that thing, I knew that I needed to keep moving forward.

## GET TO A POINT OF ACCEPTANCE . . . EVEN IF IT TAKES A MINUTE

I didn't understand until I was several years out of the NFL that when I had first retired, I had experienced some depression. It was a feeling that I hadn't had before, but I realized that the more I resisted it and the transitions that I was going through, the harder it was to break away from it. For me, this feeling was derived from an obsessive concentration on negative thoughts. The more I thought negatively about my situation, the worse it seemed to be.

Leaving the NFL, I lost my team. I felt like if I wasn't good enough to play football, then I wasn't good enough to contribute to any part of life in a meaningful way. I wanted to play a tenth season. It was a personal mark for me. In some way, after living my childhood dream for a full decade, not getting a call to play in 2013 felt like a failure. I was in a massive change looking to pivot through an emotional roller coaster. I talked with teammates and other former players, wondering if they felt the same way after leaving the game. I was surprised to learn that others were suffering too. Some had even contemplated suicide. That was a wakeup to hear words of defeat, but I can share that I too battled my own internal conflict.

Following my NFL career, I had more time than I wanted, and over time, my agent felt more and more distant. It went from updates to fewer calls to radio silence. This was uncomfortable, but what I didn't recognize is that the discomfort that I felt was denial. Change is challenging. Pivots are hard.

Eventually, after putting in a lot of effort to change my thought patterns, I began to accept my new role. I began to see myself differently. I began to see a new identity that went way beyond Jordan in a jersey. Once I was comfortable in my new Ground Zero, I started enjoying covering the league. I toured stadiums across the country, got to meet fans who were loyal to different teams all across the country. I even got to like living in downtown Los Angeles.

But not long after I settled into my new role, things changed again. After three years, *NFL AM* was canceled. It was time to pivot again.

# ✕ PIVOT TO WIN
# CHAPTER 11 RECAP

Although I struggled with my most significant pivot, from playing in the NFL to being an analyst who commented on it, good things can come from change. As you move from one chapter of your life into another, commit to seeing the positive things that come from transition. You can do this by:

1) **Asking for What You Want**
   There is no time like the present to ask for what you want. Yes, asking for what you want can be intimidating, but nothing wrong ever comes from it. You may not get what you want, but you will discover something else if you don't. Write a list of the things that you want for yourself, your family, and your career. Then think about who you can ask or connect with that might be able to provide either guidance or opportunity. Finally, act!

2) **Letting Hindsight Be Your Guide**
   Take a few minutes to write down some of your greatest life accomplishments. These accomplishments might include when one of your children was born, an award, a career milestone, or even something that you did that positively impacted another person's life. These memories will show you that grit and determination already exist within you. Use these examples to move you into the future.

3) **Understanding That Acceptance Is Your Companion**
   Acceptance can be difficult, but it can bring peace. You will experience struggle, but this doesn't mean settling for your current position. It can be helpful to speak with a professional when experiencing disruptive pivots in life.

"It's not the big things that add up in the end; it's the hundreds, thousands, or millions of little things that separate the ordinary from the extraordinary."

—Darren Hardy

# YOU CANNOT DENY ME

✕

'm not exactly sure why *NFL AM* went on hiatus. There are a million reasons a show can get canceled, including changes in upper management or issues with viewership and advertising. All I know is that one day I was told it was the last show and that was that. I was already exploring opportunities to leverage new ideas. I went back to Seattle, reached out to the Seahawks to explore the chances of joining the broadcast team to provide game-day analyst work. Before I knew it, I was into my second stint with the same franchise that gave me a chance as a player. If I had reacted differently when my time as a Seahawks player was coming to an end, I'm not sure the team would have treated me the same.

I started thinking about the things I'm good at, the things that interest me, and the things that would fit with my values. There was a definite shift in mindset for me during this process, and I went back to how it started as a kid. I recognized that to pivot successfully, I needed to go back to training camp: school. I began taking classes in accounting, film, and TV production, and eventually enrolled in the Leadership Executive MBA program at the Albers School of Business and Economics at Seattle University. I desperately wanted to increase my skill in corporate leadership as well as learn additional skills that would help me run a profitable business.

I also helped start our second company, Assure Ride, a transportation provider with private chauffeur service and scheduled medical transports. Talk about a pivot! I went from being one of the best in the world to a novice that needed to develop a whole host of new skills to succeed.

## FROM CELEBRITY TO COMMUNITY

Starting Assure Ride meant a way of giving back, a core value embedded in me by Mama. Giving back builds community. When my dad died, I was very young, but Mom always ensured that my siblings and I cared for each other. She created a community for us and that was a large part of my upbringing. The community helped raise me, helped teach me values, and helped me work my way into the NFL. It was the community that helped Mama get through her biggest pivot—learning to raise five kids by herself. We grew up in a city where 30 percent of the population lived in poverty, and we watched Mama scrape pennies and do whatever she had to do to fight the negative influences that could have easily derailed any of us. I was raised to respect and serve community.

The idea to start Assure Ride happened after being introduced to the medical transport industry by a family friend. I started researching the benefits a service like Assure Ride could provide for vulnerable populations and decided to move forward with it.

In Section 1, I mentioned approaching new things like a clock. Understanding how each function within any system moves and supports other pieces in the system is a challenge, but I was up for the challenge. I began scrolling my contacts to leverage local relationships. I identified specific events to create buzz and visibility and joined regional and national networking groups. It was a big net to cast, but I had a lot to discover, considering my lack of experience in that field. The biggest quality I have is figuring things out, even when failure is a threat.

---------------------------------------------

## The biggest quality I have is figuring things out, even when failure is a threat.

---------------------------------------------

Nearly every part of starting a new company was challenging. I had to learn about transportation, employment laws, how to help health care plans build patient retention, and how to put forth competitive bids for large national health care companies. I studied other companies to understand their operations, marketing strategies, systems processes, risk management—all the way down to how to build an effective culture. Just like my childhood discovery of the clock, in business everything operates as a system. Building a sustainable business that functions greatly depends on how well you run systems.

Following that realization, I started outsourcing numerous supportive services. Then I started identifying the customer groups that suffered the most from transportation barriers and developed a plan for reaching them. The bottleneck of our growth happened when I tried to assume each of these roles. I even drove passengers to appointments and then processed their payments in the evening. This wasn't my vision of starting a new company, and I needed help if Assure Ride was going to reach its full potential.

Since I started Assure Ride, every day has been one of discovery. As my mentor, Darren Hardy, mentioned in *The Entrepreneur Roller Coaster,* "You can't ride the entrepreneur roller coaster and stay the same. You'll become smarter, more resilient." Some days I would meet with advisors to create tax strategy as part of business planning; other times it was government compliance, business loans, developing hiring processes, or looking at the liability coverage needed to transport passengers. If there was a book for how to start a business, I didn't make it past the page that said, "That's a good idea, you should do it!"

At first, I wanted to build the whole enterprise by myself. I made a pretty good attempt, but it wasn't sustainable. No one man can achieve great things alone, as I know from my days on football teams—business is a team sport too!

Most companies struggle to make a profit in the early stages. During Assure Ride's first few years, a lot of money went out without much coming in. The beginning stages of developing the company focused on setup costs, training and safety programs, liability, and certifications, yet I kept going.

One lesson I learned from Jim Rohn is that "life is a constant quest of figuring things out." Life is an aspect of trial and error. When the odds were stacked against me, I revisited the beginning of my football career. If you think about it, I was once again in the same position—an underdog looking to get into the fight. Finding banking partners was a challenge considering the potential risk. I often found myself caught between a great idea and passion for helping people and limited financial capacity to achieve it. This fueled me.

There are a lot of similarities between running a business and running a well-executed football play. Everyone must perform their role. To do that, they must practice to build confidence, constantly looking for ways to improve. In business, the objective requires a different skill set than dodging a 300-pound lineman while trying to make a tackle, but the work ethic is the same. As author Michael Gerber says, "Everything we know how to do is tested by everything we don't know how to do." A growth mindset is required.

## FOCUS OUTSIDE OF YOURSELF

As any entrepreneur will tell you, it's completely normal to bounce around numerous ideas before settling on a new business.

Regardless of the ideas that I had, I kept returning to two questions:

- → What product or service can I provide that helps many people?
- → How can I create and build community and philanthropic initiatives while also generating income for my family?

The shift toward a service mindset wasn't a big change for me, as I still continue to volunteer and donate to charitable causes. The shift was becoming more intentional in this. We live at a time when the world needs change. When I played in the NFL, I was focused on me. I always looked for the competitive advantage and, because of that, was truly focused on the self. Think about it. Each athlete is expected to perform at a certain level and if you aren't eating, resting, or recovering properly, it could affect game performance. Once I was away from the game for a few years and had more time to slow down, I was able to reconnect with the gratitude for the opportunities that had been awarded to me. I wanted to find a way to give back to others who maybe weren't able to do the same.

Socially, we are taught to wake up every day and move our needle forward: Set a new goal. Achieve a new goal. Buy more things. Be careful using the gathering of things as your gauge for success. The measurement of who you become in the process of achieving what you want will far exceed the reward of the achievement. The reward is nothing more than a way to commemorate a moment in time.

---

> The measurement of who you become in the process of achieving what you want will far exceed the reward of the achievement.

---

## EVERYONE WILL FAIL

Before I started Assure Ride, I experienced my share of business failures. First, in 2005 right after I was drafted by the Atlanta Falcons, Monsta and I invested in a restaurant that eventually closed its doors. Five years after the restaurant's doors closed, we launched a new business that invested in film and TV productions. We were only focused on low-budget productions of less than $1 million. It was a new industry and we were fortunate to be a part of successful productions of urban comedy content working with Kevin Hart, Mike Epps, and other talented comedians and actors. I even met the "Big Aristotle" Shaquille O'Neal, backstage at the All-Star Comedy Jam in Dallas. Less than a year later, we stepped outside of the low-budget production market and increased our production investment budget. It was a bigger risk, but it warranted bigger returns too. We made it to the big screens. I, along with my brother, was juggling performing at a high level every week on the football field, while guarding business opportunities against crumbling. After all, it was the biggest investment we made since starting our company. "We just want to hit singles," we'd say to low-risk business deals. But this time, we swung to hit the home run and nearly lost the entire company. We could not have predicted the film would be mismanaged by the parties in charge of delivering the final product. Monsta and I were in the middle of our football careers. I was in my first season with the Titans, and big bro was thriving as a team leader and locker room captain in Atlanta. On our playing field of business, you can say we were placed on the injured reserve list. It took several years to recover investment dollars, and it left the company dissipated.

The point is, you can't just walk into something that's new and expect not to experience some shortcomings. I wish it were easy and no one failed. But failure is also a drive that can separate those who think from those who do. As Michael Jordan, my all-time favorite basketball player, said, "Failure is acceptable. Everyone fails at something, but I cannot accept not trying."

As I navigated the biggest pivot of my life, each "failure" helped me gain personal perspective. Now, however, I am in the transformation stage of my pivot. I know if you are doing the work within your life to establish a successful pivot, you'll move into the transformation stage too.

## PIVOTS CAN BE DISRUPTIVE

The entire world pivoted in 2020 due to the COVID-19 pandemic. Everyone was forced to pivot, both personally and professionally. The normalcy of routine, as once known, was no more. Political officials and health care experts scrambled to suppress the spread of the virus through mandated shutdowns, which overnight changed every part of how we live. Thousands of companies went out of business, people unexpectedly lost loved ones, and small-business owners, like me, either went under, increased their debt, or capitalized on the opportunities presented by a volatile marketplace. To this day, recovery has been challenging and people are still pivoting. The disruption of the 2020 pandemic threatens to widen the racial homeownership and employment gap between Black and white Americans. Job cuts across the world reached astronomical numbers, the volume of unemployment claims in the U.S. peaked to nearly 15 percent, and suddenly, temperature checks and face masks became necessary when entering businesses, airports, and public settings.

## RESPECT YOUR RESILIENCY

Each of us is resilient and each of us chooses whether to feed or starve that resiliency. U.S. Navy Seal Commander Mark Divine calls it "staring down your fear wolf." When we face our deep negative qualities and stare them down, we overcome the negative impact they can have on our life. When we feed our resiliency, there's no stopping us. When we starve it, we rob ourselves of the endless possibilities in our lives. Think back to a time when you experienced friction in pursuit of something you wanted but elected to take the easy route. Now think of a time you pushed through that friction to get what you wanted. These two scenarios have happened to all of us, and each of us has either built that muscle of resiliency or starved it. When faced with a decision to pursue the challenge or not, we can choose to be something more or stay the same. We can choose to leave a legacy that exceeds our time on Earth. I know I want that and if you've made it this far with me on this journey, I know you do too.

------------------------------------------------

When we feed our resiliency, there's no stopping us. When we starve it, we rob ourselves of the endless possibilities in our lives.

------------------------------------------------

## TAKE CARE OF YOURSELF

As you pivot through life, vitality is essential. Has a planned or unplanned change happened recently? How has it affected your mental and physical state? Remember, the anchor of your pivot is you, and you must take time for yourself. During my time in the NFL, I spent a lot of time taking care of my mind and body. I did not like sitting in forty-degree water up to my waist, but I needed to flush out any lactic acid and muscle soreness to have fresh legs for game day. While I put my body under enormous physical stress, I also knew that how well I took care of my psyche was equally important.

Recently, I added ten minutes of meditation—quiet time, think time, whatever you call it—to my daily routine. It's a moment to be still. Does it work for everyone? Maybe not, but it's worth a try. I have found that these practices help generate energy and increase mental and physical strength.

→ Add Meditation—a moment of quiet, daily
→ Change Daily Interactions—have better conversations, increase relationships even if it means joining a volunteer group
→ Shut Down Earlier—get your rest
→ Practice Presence—stop multitasking so much
→ Wellness Check—On a scale of 1 to 10, how would you rate your diet, rest, and activity level?

You may not be an NFL player, but athletes are just like everyone else. We have to learn to take care of our bodies and minds so that we can achieve maximum performance. My experiences will be different from yours, but the process of pivoting is similar. Take some time to embrace how the model fits you, put one foot in front of the other, and keep moving in the direction of your goal.

# ✕------- PIVOT TO WIN -------
# CHAPTER 12 RECAP

Pivoting takes a little time, a little self-reflection, and a lot of patience. After all, most pivots are a practice of reinventing yourself. After making several of my own pivots, these are the elements of reinvention that were most useful for me:

### 1) Looking Outside of Myself

If you're having a hard time moving on from obsessing about your own problems, look outside of yourself. What can you do within your community to help those who are facing struggles that are worse than your own? Not only does looking outside of yourself reframe your thought process and make you feel good, it can also lead to new ideas for your own life.

### 2) Employing Both a Growth and Service Mindset

Nothing can be lost when we commit to growing and serving. What can you do today to grow as a person? A parent? A professional? Who in your life has a growth mindset? Can you sit down with them and talk about how they maintain that mindset? As for a service mindset, what can you offer others even when you're struggling? What skill sets do you have that you can lend to someone else?

### 3) Focusing on Leadership

You don't have to run a company or be an elected official to lead. Each of us has the opportunity to lead every single day, be it how we are as a parent, how we are as a spouse, or how we are in our job. Find a leadership style that you admire and then learn from the leaders who operate based on that style of leadership. Read the books they've written and listen to the interviews they've given. Commit to becoming your own leader.

>

"The first step toward creating
an improved future is developing
the ability to envision it."

—Tony Dungy

# CHAPTER 13

# PIVOT TO WIN WITH THE PIVOT MODEL

✕

Pivoting can be broken down into minuscule pieces with the Pivot Model.

1) **Recognize.**

Find a favorable way to leverage your relationships, position, or skill set into more opportunity.

2) **Decide.**

Commit to process. All in or all out. This is a good place to tap into your community of like-minded people.

3) **Find Ground Zero.**

This is your new normal, a time to stop, reflect, and think about your next step. When you claim the new normal, new skills and gifts will emerge. Personal values will guide this phase.

4) **Be Courageous.**

Persisting is simply wanting something greater than the circumstance. Life is a journey that is sometimes uncomfortable, but incremental steps in the midst of discomfort grow into new insights. There's no telling how much you can achieve if you act today.

5) **Transform.**

When you reach a deeper awareness and move through change, you will feel connected to your purpose. The conversion of the pivot is who we become in the process.

The pivot model leads us to a place of acceptance. Whether you intentionally plan your pivot or something out of your control forces you to pivot, you have to acknowledge your new reality or you will experience friction.

Take what happened in 2020 when COVID-19 disrupted the global economy. Everyone was forced to pivot personally and professionally. There is loss in change, but new habits can be programmed through behavioral change. When we recognize certain triggers that influence the way we think or act, we can control the way we behave. I wouldn't expect you to apply this thought process to losing a loved one or a dramatic or near-death emotional experience. Grieving takes time and sometimes requires professional help. I am talking about our current state, which for all of us means a change in economy, losing a job, making a career change, or starting a new business. Right now, change—and pivoting because of it—is unavoidable.

When external change happens, internal change must follow because no matter how many times you try, a square peg will not fit into a round hole. Not unless you melt the steel and change its structure.

# DEVELOP YOUR PIVOT PLAN TO WIN

We've gone through thirteen chapters of work! Now that I've shared how I've pivoted, let's get you doing the same with these 37 action items.

1) **Embrace Struggle**

Every day we face challenges, some big, some small. Think of a time when you have faced a challenge or adversity head on. Now think of a time when you didn't. How did you feel after each situation? How would you act differently if you faced a challenge today?

## 2) Have a Little Faith

I know it's not in everyone's nature to have faith in something greater than themselves, but no matter who you are, you have to have faith in something. Otherwise, what's the point? At the very least, have faith in yourself.

## 3) Find Your Own Strengths

Self-identity is powerful. Find your own strengths for yourself, not for other people. Talk to yourself like you're talking to your best friend. How do you describe yourself? What strengths do you list? What would your best friend, mother, or anyone else who supports and loves you add to that list?

## 4) Find People Who Will Hold You Accountable

I don't mean find people who support your bad habits. Find the ones that support your good habits and push you to develop new habits. Ask yourself, Who do I know who lives a life that I want to live? Who around me has a set of morals that I would like to mirror? Then interview these people. How do they live? How can you act in a similar way? What kind of actions can the two of you take to hold each other accountable to your goals?

## 5) Visualize What You Want from Your Own Life

Find images that support that vision and put them up in your office or home. Envision acting as the person you want to become. Use images, audio, and words to reinforce what you want to do in life. The power of visualizing your path will help reinforce good decisions and minimize your chances of making mistakes.

## 6) Learn from Your Mistakes

Think about a choice you've made that doesn't align with the person you want to become. What can you do to prevent yourself from being in that situation again? Who can you rely on to help you stay out of toxic environments? What do you need to change?

# PIVOT 2 WIN
## DISCOVERY PROCESS

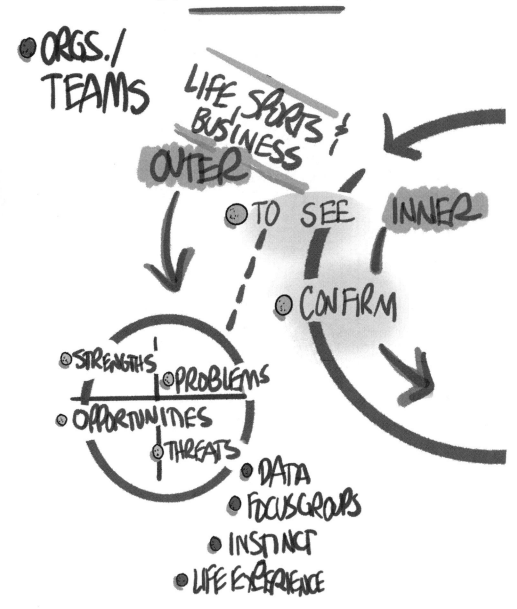

ORGS./TEAMS

LIFE SPORTS & BUSINESS

OUTER

TO SEE

INNER

CONFIRM

STRENGTHS

PROBLEMS

OPPORTUNITIES

THREATS

DATA
FOCUS GROUPS
INSTINCT
LIFE EXPERIENCE

- INDIVIDUALS
  - WHO WE BECOME IN PROCESS

- DEEPER AWARENESS
- INSIGHT INTO WHAT'S NEXT

- SUPPORTING A NEW IDENTITY

- LIVING IN PURPOSE

- RECONNECT TO PURPOSE

- PERSIST COURAGEOUSLY
  - A QUEST
  - INTENTION
  - DISCOMFORT
  - INCREMENTAL STEPS

- RELAUNCH STAY ENGAGED
- "HOLD FAST"

- ACT
  - PHYSICAL
  - EMOTIONAL
  - SPIRITUAL
  - ORG. CULTURE

7) **Welcome New Levels of Competition**
Competition not only offers the ability to gauge your skills but also pushes you to elevate your game. Life will present opportunities that challenge you to do things before you are ready. The greatest teacher is experience. Welcome the new level of competition. Your breakthrough of confidence awaits your brave intentions.

8) **Embrace Internal Competition**
Never stop competing against yourself. Only you know if you performed your best. Remember to block external triggers. You control your actions, behaviors, and habits.

9) **Get Out of Your Way**
Playing or living for yourself can be limiting. Go outside yourself to compete for something greater than you. Whether pursuing the best grade in your class, becoming the top salesperson in your company, or scoring the game-winning points, the pursuit of your desires must be stronger than the roadblocks set to stop you.

10) **Challenge Yourself**
Anyone who wants more for themselves must grow themselves first. I sought out the opportunity to train at the next level. You too must seek out trainings, seminars, and coaching relative to your desires. This has helped me increase my skills and chance to win. You can hit your goals by surrounding yourself with other like-minded people who inspire.

11) **Refuse to Take "No" for an Answer**
When I face a "no," it means I've asked the wrong person. Sometimes the person who says no doesn't even have authority. My stubbornness won't let me walk away without seeking the person who has the "yes" that I'm looking for. "No" could be the one thing standing between you and achieving your goal. Consider this approach the next time someone tells you no.

12) **View the End Game as a Clock**
Everything has a system. To crack the system, you have to break it apart. Start to understand how things work. If you're mindful of

how one thing affects the other, it can be your advantage. Think of one goal you want to achieve. What areas have the greatest impact? What are the biggest influencers of these areas? When you continue to ask questions, you will dissect the process and make the next best strategic move.

### 13) Accept That There's More Than One Way

Just because the path to your goal looks different than those before you doesn't mean you won't get to your finish line. Challenges will happen, but a defensive back mentality can help keep you moving forward. Examine where you are and be courageous enough to move through change. What do you need to accept to overcome a situation? Can a routine help you regain control in your life?

### 14) Create the Life You Want

I don't know a single person who is living the life they want who got there by sitting on the couch. You must actively go after whatever it is that you want every single day. Win the day to gain momentum and start living the life you want.

### 15) Know That Someone's Always Watching

Even when you think no one is paying attention, someone is always watching, which means you always have to be on point. This isn't about being perfect. It's about being consistent and intentional. Do not let your foot off the gas. Whatever you want in life, you can accomplish it. What do you do to stay on point? Have you considered an accountability person or group to keep you focused?

### 16) Cultivate Persistence

We will face challenges. When we act with bold intentions and pursue our goals with courage, each obstacle will become a stepping-stone. The step to the next level is in your next challenge! This is the perfect opportunity to prevail.

### 17) Persevere in the Face of Obstacles

You're going to meet obstacles in your journey toward success. Understand that and then develop an attitude and mental state that will allow you to face those obstacles without backing down.

18) **Do It Now**

Remember, "later" is a dream killer. Success leaves clues if you are observant. Where can you learn something from observing others? Are you the best you can become? Draw the line and make the change today. Get ready to pivot. Make the decision today; don't wait. There are no shortcuts. The only way forward is to do it now!

19) **Appreciate the Sandwich**

Just when you think you've got it all figured out, life will humble you. It takes a level of maturity to notice those moments and appreciate them as reminders that we are all human. So grab that PB&J with a slice of humble pie and take a moment to reflect.

20) **Practice Humility**

Humility is an admirable quality. When we dismiss our self-pride and narcissist ideals, we can see more clearly. This clarity will be invaluable when you need to pivot from a position in which you were comfortable—whether voluntarily or involuntarily.

21) **Think Outside of Yourself**

A serve-first approach is one way to put others first. It removes the feeling of entitlement. The reciprocity of helping others cannot be measured. What skills do you have that you can share with others who are struggling?

22) **Understand Your Vulnerability**

When we pivot, we move from a familiar place to an uncertain one. As a result, we can feel unsettled and vulnerability can creep in. When did you last feel vulnerable? How did you handle those emotions? If the outcome wasn't your expectation, was it hard to accept? Remember, vulnerability means being receptive, open to new ideas. What would you like to do differently the next time you're in a vulnerable place?

23) **Be Emotionally Resilient**

When you're in a vulnerable place, take a moment to look at the situation logically. Emotions can cloud our thinking, but when we act in accord with our personal values, it's liberating. Master the things you can control. It's okay to feel the emotions of life, but it's another thing to let them dictate your behavior. Challenges demand for us to self-examine. What can you learn from this experience? What about the situation can you control? Whatever you can't control, it's time to let go of.

## 24) Grab Your Helmet

Equip yourself as best you can to meet the challenges of change and pivot to win. Identify your weaknesses in your vulnerable moments and use this time to grow. Lean into your strengths and put your best performance forward.

## 25) Accept Change

We know change is our only constant, but we can pivot to win when we create new favorable situations by using leverage. How do you react to change? Do you embrace it with an optimistic mindset or does it leave you feeling stuck? Build on your past engagements when dealing with change to help guide you.

## 26) Understand That Open Options = Innovation

Move through your pivot with an open mind. Be creative in finding ways to position yourself for a win. Reach out to your support network, and don't be afraid to make new connections in pursuit of possibilities.

## 27) Focus on What's Ahead

Whatever we focus on gets our attention. Life is a magnifying glass that can burn a hole in a piece of paper when it's in pure focus. You too can ignite a fire when you focus on what's in front of you. Stare into the rearview mirror too long and you'll crash. Get back in the game and pursue the future you really want.

## 28) Don't Stay Stuck

You can feel stuck, you can complain about being stuck, but once the emotion passes, get to work! Focus on finding resources that are uplifting and give you hope. Be kind to yourself and focus on the image of your better self. When days don't feel great, go to paradise. Train your mind to think about greatness. Beating yourself up won't get you anywhere.

**29) Be Vulnerable**

Are there areas in your life that feel guarded? To be vulnerable means to challenge our insecurities. When we explore these thoughts of self-doubt, it's crucial to understand how they make us think. Sometimes the feeling of embarrassment can be the reason to drive change. Remember, we are moving toward the best version of you. Take an honest inventory of areas to prune, and ask others for help.

**30) Examine Your Behaviors**

Change is constant. We must be intentional about growing ourselves, even during a pivot. Consider developing new skills and new relationships that support your discoveries in Ground Zero. The first step to change is looking at your behaviors. What activities do you do in a day, a week, or a month? Once you create a list of those behaviors, it will be easier to see what stays and what goes. Which of these activities is serving you? Which will you give up in pursuit of something more? Find your balance.

**31) Trust the Process**

I have used failure as a stepping-stone to reach new levels. Small setbacks happen, but don't beat yourself up over it. Learn from them. Each obstacle builds resilience and belief. You are not the same person today as you were yesterday. You will not be the same person one year from today. Let's continue the journey together.

**32) Ask for What You Want**

There is no time like the present to ask for what you want. Yes, asking for what you want can be intimidating, but nothing wrong ever comes from it. You may not get what you want, but you will discover something else if you don't. Write a list of the things you want for yourself, your family, and your career. Then think about who you can ask or connect with that might be able to either provide guidance or opportunity. Finally, act!

**33) Let Hindsight Be Your Guide**

Take a few minutes to write down some of your greatest life accomplishments. These accomplishments might include when one of your children was born, an award, a career milestone, or even something that you did that positively impacted another person's life. These memories will show you that grit and determination already exist within you. Use these examples to move you into the future.

### 34) Understand That Acceptance Is Your Companion
Acceptance can be difficult, but it can bring peace. You will experience struggle, but this doesn't mean settling for your current position. It can be helpful to speak with a professional when experiencing disruptive pivots in life.

### 35) Look Outside of Yourself
If you're having a hard time moving on from obsessing about your own problems, look outside of yourself. What can you do within your community to help those who are facing struggles worse than your own? Not only does looking outside of yourself reframe your thought process and make you feel good, but also it can lead to new ideas for your own life.

### 36) Employ Both a Growth and a Service Mindset
Nothing can be lost when we commit to growing and serving. What can you do today to grow as a person? A parent? A professional? Who in your life has a growth mindset? Can you sit down with them and talk about how they maintain that mindset? As for a service mindset, what can you offer others even when you're struggling? What skill sets do you have that you can lend to someone else?

### 37) Focus on Leadership
You don't have to run a company or be an elected official to lead. Each of us has the opportunity to lead every single day, be it how we are as a parent, how we are as a spouse, or how we are in our job. Find a leadership style that you admire and then learn from the leaders who operate based on that style. Read the books they've written and listen to the interviews they've given. Commit to becoming your own leader.

T hank you for sharing this journey with me! Now that you have your Pivot Playbook, I know that you're going to get out there and crush the week!

I hope my experiences, successes, failures, and missteps have given you helpful tools that you'll be able to apply to your own life. Each of us has desires, but very few of us commit to taking the steps needed to pursue our aspirations. But you're here, right now, finishing this book, which tells me that you have the capacity to pivot—and pivot well. There's no telling what you can achieve when you persist, and you have to persist because life is never going to stop throwing you pivots.

Where I compete has pivoted—it's no longer on the football field—but I am still hungry to reach new levels in life. I want more in my relationships, finances, business ventures, spirituality, and health. I want better and am always looking to learn and grow as I did as an athlete, and I want the same for you. But better doesn't come easily. You and I both know that. Better requires work even when that work is slow, boring, and mundane. However, if there's one thing that life's pivots have taught me, it's that they offer more space for growth and change than achievement ever could. When you set a goal, it's the journey that makes getting there worthwhile. Once you hit that goal, new ambitions arise. Then the pursuit begins again, and again, and again. When you embrace your pivots, pursuit never ends. It becomes your life.

The Jordan of twenty years ago was all about football. How to play it, how to master it, and then how to beat the odds to get paid to play it. As you've seen throughout *Pivot to Win*, I learned many things from my unrelenting goal to become a professional football player. I learned what is possible when a person is relentless to win. I learned how to create my own opportunities while also learning how to structure my pivots.

All good things come to an end. It doesn't matter what field you're in, where you're from, or what your background is. Life constantly asks each of us to pivot and transition. I was fortunate to play professional sports and am thankful for every experience and relationship that came from it. But I'm also aware that the constant in life is change. If you're at the top right now, know that you won't always be. Someone with the same ambition that got you to the top will chase their passion just like you did until they're on top. Conversely, if you're at the bottom, know that you don't have to stay there. One of the beautiful things about change is that it allows us to reinvent ourselves. But we can only do this by growing. If you want more, become more. Embrace your pivots. View them not as something to fear but as incentives to keep growing.

Although I experienced struggles in life, sports, and business, my failures became stepping-stones. I failed my way to success during each of my pivots. By showing how I've done things, my goal is to help you understand and navigate change better so that you can pivot to win!

Now it's your turn. The life you want to live is hidden in the daily choices you make. Success is yours, and there's more than one way to meet it. Go forth, pivot, and win.

Sincerely,

*Jordan Babineaux*

Jordan Babineaux

# ACKNOWLEDGMENTS

Since my early youth, football has been a part of many lessons and contributions to my life. To this day, thanks to football, I push my physical limits and challenge my mental capacity. Playing sports started as an escape from the pains of my youth—dealing with the early loss of Dad, escaping the streets and dead-end paths—and ended up becoming a staple in developing adversity quotient (AQ). Life for each of us is full of adversities, but the ability to deal with those challenges fueled me to see them as opportunities.

This book would not be possible without the many people who have impacted my life. When I started on the journey to write this book, I did not know how much mental, emotional, and physical endurance it would take. Nor did I know that I would meet an incredible group of people who have added value to me and have great intentions to do good in our world.

The journey to the National Football League (NFL) took many people to help us along the way—family friends who were there to assist, the elders of the church who kept us covered in prayer, and the entire city of Port Arthur—to reach such a noble accomplishment.

Writing a book while attaining an executive MBA degree has been as challenging as any obstacle I've faced in life or the NFL. It's allowed me to self-reflect and focus my lens inward. The clasp of honing new skills through a transformational course of study caused me to interrogate areas in my life that were calloused by personal experience. I was moved to tears, unaware it would be a revelation for me.

My mother deserves the accolades for navigating the ship through uncertain times. In our toughest time, you demonstrated persistence, discipline, and unwavering faith. Thanks, Mama.

To my wife, Everly, and my kids, Jaida, Joseph, and Jace, thank you for giving me space to go after ambitious goals while pursuing life's greater purpose. You are as important to this journey as I am.

To my brothers and sisters, Joseph, Shan, Jeffery, Joshua, and Jean, who each taught me valuable life lessons and set the standard to follow. I learned a lot from watching you and, without a doubt, it expanded the vision for myself.

To my brother and best friend, Monsta, words cannot express my gratitude for our story. You make me better in life.

To my mentor, Darren Hardy, who challenges me to be the exception. You have my greatest appreciation for our daily mentor chats, and encouraging me to write this book.

Turning an idea into a book is as hard as it sounds. The experience is internally rewarding and challenging. I especially want to thank the individuals who helped make this happen.

Reed Bilbray, your brilliant ideas and expertise in our mastermind sessions were significant to this process. You bring an ability to orchestrate a complex compilation with ease.

It is a joy to work with you, Ivy Hughes. Every day for the last sixteen months, you were there to push my writing capacity far past my comfort. Your pursuit to bring ideas into words was ingenious.

Kim Baker, the greatest cover designer I could imagine, your creativity and meticulous approach made the intense writing process a seamless assembly.

Working with you, Tim Corey, has been a feeling of enlightenment. From the first day we met, our road map exercises have given a clear direction as I redefine success. I am grateful for your illustrations to this book and contribution to my leadership journey.

Many elements developed the book content, and I am grateful for those who took the time to offer a review, collaborate, and share distinct perspectives, including Alyssa Rabins and Lorrie Baldevia. Thank you for the extra set of eyes and feedback.

To my team, Rick Brown, Jason Orton, Kere Greene, and Heather Clancy, thank you for your input and teamwork. Especially, LeAnne Dolce, for sharing your creative input, not only to this book and web design but also personally and professionally. I respect and appreciate each of you.

To each of the members of our Seattle University Leadership Executive MBA cohort, thank you for letting me share stories, exchange ideas, and navigate through the grind of this achievement. It would not have been possible without your teamwork.

To Coach Rhodes, for never letting me get comfortable, and all of my coaches and teammates over the years—Little League Football, Woodrow Middle School, Lincoln High School, Southern Arkansas, Seattle Seahawks, and Tennessee Titans—thank you for pushing me to be a great teammate and challenging me to do things that felt unimaginable.

Finally, to all those who have been a part of my adventure, said something encouraging to me, or taught me something. I heard it all, and it means a lot.

Most of all, thank God.

# RESOURCES

## READ

*Coach Wooden's Leadership Game Plan for Success* by John Wooden and
   Steve Jamison
*The Compound Effect* by Darren Hardy
*The Extraordinary Power of Leader Humility* by Marilyn Gist, Ph.D.
*Fierce Conversations* by Susan Scott
*How to Be an Antiracist* by Ibram Kendi
*The ONE Thing* by Gary Keller and Jay Papasan
*Relentless: From Good to Great to Unstoppable* by Tim Grover
*Start with Why* by Simon Sinek
*Staring Down the Wolf* by Mark Divine
*Switch* by Chip Heath and Dan Heath
*The Power of Habit* by Charles Duhigg
*High Performance Habits* by Brendon Burchard
*Work Is Love Made Visible* by Frances Hesselbein
*Leading An Inspired Life* by Jim Rohn

## LISTEN/WATCH

*The Mind of Kobe Bryant—Obsession* by Kobe Bryant
*The Mindset of a Winner* by Kobe Bryant
*The Strangest Secret* by Earl Nightingale
*University of Texas 2014 Commencement Speech* by Admiral William McRaven

# THE AUTHOR

Jordan Babineaux transitioned from nearly a decade playing in the NFL to become a sports broadcaster, entrepreneur, and business executive. Jordan helps companies, teams, athletes, and young adults navigate their pivots.

Jordan holds a bachelor's degree in mass communication from Southern Arkansas University and a Leadership Executive MBA from Seattle University. During his college football career, Jordan earned NCAA All-American First-Team honors as a cornerback and was inducted into the SAU Hall of Fame in 2018.

Signed to the NFL as an undrafted free agent, Babineaux worked his way up to starting as a defensive back for the Seattle Seahawks, playing in Super Bowl XL. In his seven years playing for the Seahawks, he earned the nickname "Big Play Babs" for making several game-changing plays.

After signing with the Tennessee Titans, Jordan played two more seasons before retiring with over 140 career games in the NFL.

Jordan then pivoted from the NFL to sports broadcasting, regularly appearing on the NFL Network's morning show *NFL AM*. Today, Jordan provides commentary and analysis for the Seahawks game day radio and TV broadcasts. He continues to give back to the game of football, helping rookies prepare for life in the NFL and athletes who transition out of sports. Jordan also acts as a player advisor to the most extensive study ever conducted of living former players, the Football Players Health Study at Harvard University.

As an entrepreneur, Jordan has experience in a variety of fields. Along with his brother Jonathan Babineaux, former defensive end for the Atlanta Falcons, Jordan started 2 Brothers Productions. Their company produced several stand-up comedy specials for stars such as Kevin Hart and Mike Epps. He also founded Assure Ride, a company that combines his business skills with his desire to serve the community by providing black car and private transportation services.

Jordan believes giving back to the community is one of the most important things he can do in life. He and his brother Jonathan founded the Babineaux Family Foundation, a nonprofit that gives back to their hometown of Port Arthur, Texas, and the Seattle, Washington, and Atlanta, Georgia, communities.

Through his *Pivot to Win* book, his *Pivotal Moments* podcast, and other platforms, Jordan shares his journey of personal growth to help others navigate change and pivot successfully.

Jordan lives in Seattle, Washington, with his wife and three children while squeezing in a round of golf with friends as often as possible.

To book Jordan for coaching or speaking events, visit www.pivottowin.com or email speaker@pivottowin.com.

# LET'S CONNECT

## WORK WITH JORDAN TO BUILD, CONNECT & TRANSFORM YOUR TEAM TO MAKE THE BIG PLAYS

Jordan helps companies, teams, athletes, and young adults navigate their pivots. To have Jordan speak, consult or partner with your company, visit www.pivottowin.com or email speaker@pivottowin.com

### CONNECT WITH JORDAN

To get tips and insights on navigating your own pivotal moments, join Jordan's community for free by visiting www.pivottowin.com

### CONNECT WITH JORDAN ON SOCIAL MEDIA

    jordanbabineaux

### LISTEN TO JORDAN'S PIVOTAL MOMENTS PODCAST

Jordan shares stories of success and failure that will help you navigate change in your life and business. Subscribe at www.pivottowin.com/podcast

### CONNECT WITH THE BABINEAUX FAMILY FOUNDATION

The Babineaux Family Foundation is a non-profit organization designed to open doors for youth, community development and build awareness for the chronic autoimmune disease lupus. To learn more about how you or your company can help, visit www.babineauxbrothers.com

### TO BOOK JORDAN FOR COACHING OR SPEAKING EVENTS

visit www.pivottowin.com or email speaker@pivottowin.com

# PIVOT 2 WIN
## DISCOVERY PROCESS

- **ORGS./TEAMS**
- **INDIVIDUALS**
  - WHO WE BECOME IN PROCESS

**OUTER**
- LIFE SPORTS & BUSINESS

**INNER**

**TO SEE**

**CONFIRM**

- STRENGTHS
- PROBLEMS
- OPPORTUNITIES
- THREATS
  - DATA
  - FOCUS GROUPS
  - INSTINCT
  - LIFE EXPERIENCE

**LIVING IN PURPOSE**

**PERSIST COURAGEOUSLY**
- ADJUST
- INTENTION
- DISCOMFORT
- INCREMENTAL STEPS

**ACT**
- PHYSICAL
- EMOTIONAL
- SPIRITUAL
- ORG. CULTURE

- **DEEPER AWARENESS**
- **INSIGHT INTO WHAT'S NEXT**
- SUPPORTING A NEW IDENTITY
- **RECONNECT TO PURPOSE**
- **RELAUNCH / STAY ENGAGED**
- "HOLD FAST"

Colibri
ColibriFacilitation.com